Communal Riots in India

Communal Riots in India

Study of Social and Econonic Aspects

AKHILESH KUMAR

Commonwealth

Communal Riots in India

Edition : 2022

ISBN 81-7169-141-2

Published by :

COMMONWEALTH PUBLISHERS
4831/24, Prahlad Street,
Ansari Road, Darya Ganj,
New Delhi - 110002
Ph. : 23275511, 23257835
Fax : 91- 011- 23257835
e-mail : commonwealthbooks@gmail.com

Typesetting by :
Rishu Computers
Delhi

Printed at :
Roshan Offset Printers
Delhi

DEDICATED TO

All those who lost their innocent lives
in Communal Riots

Preface

Every day we talk of communalism and almost everyone is haunted by the spectre of communal violence in India throughout the ages. There was and is acute rural tension along caste and communal lines. To the social pathologists, its causes appeared to be the religious. Of late, attempts were made by the social scientists to underline the socio-economic factors responsible for this social tension. It is expected in this study to explore the material basis of the problem.

The present work is not a chronological account of communal violence in India nor does it trace the evolution of communal tension. However, to the possible extent chronology has also been maintained. I have sought to understand and interpret and expose communal riots for what it is to know what its roots and social functions were during the period of colonial rule. I have also tried to understand which aspects of India's social, economic, political and cultural life were responsible for the violence, from where it drew its social support, which sections of societies were 'represented' by it, whose interests it served, and which sections promoted and organised communal politics.

At all India plane, some works have been done by a few scholars, yet no objective study has adequately been done by the historians on communal violence. G.S. Ghurye, a well reputed sociologist in his book, 'Social Tensions in India' presented a brief history of communal tension in India but it deals mainly with chronological account of the problem. There are some other names who undertook the task of studying the causes behind communal riots, but do not sufficiently explore it.

At regional or provincial level, some significant works have been done in the present decade but Bihar remains untouched even today. It is however necessary to have a full understanding of the communal problem to see the history of the province in true perspective.

This work includes six chapters. In Chapter I, it has been attempted to explore the real nature of the problem. It is because the nature of communal riot is itself misleading. In this chapter, different theories regarding communal violence have been put and a significant distinction between communalism and communal riots have been brought.

In Chapter II, it has been tried to mention some of the major riots on an all-India scale and several instances have been brought to prove that communal riots occurred also before the coming of the British. In this chapter, the changing base of communal violence at the region-wise has been underlined.

In Chapter III, the communal history of Bihar has been traced with the objectives of seeking political connections between the political vested interests and the communal violence. Several significant issues have been raised in this chapter.

Communal riots were basically class struggle, the perverted form of it. Religion was like a cloak to conceal the rea lissues. It has been adequately dealt in Chapter IV. It has been shown that most of the riots centred round land, jobs in the Government services and the hostility arising out of trade competitions.

Communal colour was given to the conflict of purely class struggle by the vested interests. As a social class, the landlords, the buraucrats, the imperialists, the bourgeoisie and the anti-social elements have been treated in Chapter V.

It has largely been attempted to see their roles in the socio-economic structure of the society and their separate responses to the communal problem.

In Chapter VI, the colonial administration has been directly blamed for their malintentions and malfunctioning of the state power. How they manipulated the whole situation for their colonial interests, has been pinpointed in this chapter.

Now it becomes all the more necessary to acknowledge those persons who extended their kind cooperation during the course of my study. First of all I shall like to acknowledge Dr. V.C.P. Choudhary (Research Fellow, K.P. Jaysawal Institute, Patna) who provided the theme and helped me at several places.

Secondly, I owe much to Prof. R.L. Shukla (Delhi University) who encouraged me a lot when I presented a paper to the Indian History Congress (Burdwan, 1983). He was also present when I read the paper on this problem and patted me much with a group of scholars. This proved an unfailing encouragement to me. I am much indebted to Mr. Ashghar Ali Engineer (Director, Institute of Islamic Studies, Bombay) who helped me a lot through correspondence.

This work could not have been a successful attempt if I could not find a supervisor like Dr. Shiv Kumar Prasad Singh who with his scholarly insight and far-sighted vision helped me in writing and giving final shape to the work. I owe much to him.

I am equally indebted to Pratima, who sincerely helped me and kept me aloof from household affairs. What more can a scholar expect from his wife ?

Apart from these individuals, institutions too play a significant role. I am in particular indebted to Patna University Library, History Department Library, Sinha Library, Khuda Baksha Khan Library and Bihar State Archives Library. I am also grateful to the sincere members of these institutions.

AKHILESH KUMAR

Abbreviations

Jan. — January

Feb — February

Aug. — August

Sept. — September

Oct. — October

Nov. — November

Dec. — December

Govt. — Government

B.S.A. — Bihar State Archives

N.A.I. — National Archives of India

I.H.C. — Indian History Congress

Contents

Introduction

Communalism is perhaps the most serious problem facing Indian society today. Conjuncturally, its virulent forms break out sometimes here, sometimes there, hitting the headlines with varying degrees of intensity. In this way, it becomes necessary for the researchers to ponder seriously over it and find instruments to check its mushroom growth.

Communalism and communal riots may not be mistaken to be the same thing. Though for a long time, there has been a good deal of popular discussion on this very subject, which was commonly shared by the British as well as the Indian scholars. The distinction was first brought by K.B. Krishna and W.C. Smith.[1] Communalism is virtually the main ideology and communal 'politics' and basically a middle class question whereas communal riots are the main form or content of communal tension.[2]

1. K B. Krishna, *The Problem of Minorities*, (London, 1939), pp. 277-79. Also see, W.C. Smith, *Modern Islam in India*, (Lahore, 1963), pp. 194, 196-97.
2. Bipan Chandra, *Communalism in Modern India*, (New Delhi, 1984), pp. 4-5.

It has rather more historical justifications that 'Communalism is not the hangover from the past . . . it is basically a modern phenomenon.' But one can hardly believe that the significance of communal violence may not be traced back to the pre-1857 period. Professor Bipan Chandra, an historian of great repute who largely influenced the writing of history in the post-independence India maintains that 'Communal tension and riots began to occur only from the last quarter of the nineteenth century. Moreover, they did not prevail in India on a significant scale till 1946-47. The overwhelming majority of Indians especially in the rural areas, were unaffected by communal tension.'[3] Though at the same time it has been accepted that 'Communal identity and division has always pervaded Indian society. In one of his articles he further says that the significance of communal violence before communalism is wrong and rather unhistorical.'[4] Rejecting this notion it has been advanced in this work that Hindu-Muslim riot did take place even before the coming of the British and before the introduction of separate electorate.[5]

But one may bring to notice the fact that the medieval rulers did not encourage communal violence what the colonial masters had done. They did so not because they were uncivilised but because they were colonial. In medieval times, when the riots did erupt at the one or the other place, the Sultan made efforts to restore peace on account of his need of the merchants.[6]

3. Bipan Chandra, op.cit., p. 4.
4. *The Mainstream*, dated May 24, 1986, Vol. XXIV No. 38, p. 11. In the article captioned 'Communalism—The way out,' Bipan Chandra writes, "Communalism is not in the main communal riots or communal violence. Certainly communal violence is linked to communal ideology of which communal riots and other forms of communal violence is linked to communal ideology. Communal ideology can prevail even without violence, but communal violence cannot exist without communal ideology."
5. For detail see Chapter II. Several riots have been cited in this chapter.
6. G.S. Ghurye, *Social Tensions in India*, (Bombay, 1968), p. 304.

Communal riots is very often a blanket term oversimplifying a variety of complexities. It often conjures up a picture of ugly mob violence sparked off exclusively by base criminality and *blind religious hostility*. The inexorable recurrence of such a phenomenon is often used to prove a fundamental incompatibility between two religious communities. This popular notion apart, historians have also attempted to explain communal violence in our country during British rule by referring to the political calculations of the leaders of the two major communities who allegedly incited such clashes to pressurise the Government before some impending constitutional readjustment.[7] But apart from such external manipulations, the riots themselves have been seen as the compound of rank criminal instincts and religious prejudices.

Apart from providing religious answer to the communal problem, it has been attempted in this work to explore the class-base character of communal violence. At every stage of social development, division along class lines has marked its existence. Karl Marx seems more objective when he writes that ". . . the history of hitherto existing society is the history of class struggle." It is to say the least that tension ever persisted in the society consequent to the opposition led by the exploited masses against the exploiters. The oppressed, exploited and unprivileged masses have always joined the forces against oppression. But such popular resentment of the masses could often find solace in the one or the other form of perversion. Communal problem is also the perverted form of class struggle.[8]

If one looks into antiquity, may point out that in ancient India the open revolt by the 'Sudras' who were chiefly

7. Reaction to the constitutional changes has been accepted as the determining factor by J.H. Broomfield in 'The Forgotten Majority —The Bengali Muslims'.

   See M. Hasan (ed), *Communal and Pan Islamic Trends in Colonial India*, (Delhi, 1981), p. 302.

8. Bipan Chandra, op.cit., p. 30.

peasants or workers, against the domination of the 'Brahmanas' and the 'Kshatriyas' who formed privileged section in the social hierarchy, was basically seen in caste and communal term. Even the 'Dharmashastras' maintain that 'the low caste people fought against the upper caste' and not that the poor peasantry revolted against the ruling elites.

In modern India, these significant developments can be marked easily. Almost every struggle along class line takes shape of a caste and communal conflict due to the imperfect politicisation of the people. One peculiar feature of the post-nineteenth century political developments is that from this period communal violence became spasmodic and recurrent. It was because the rulers themselves nourished, fed, encouraged and even instigated communal violence in their vested class interest. They accentuated the divisions already existing in the society and displayed it in their own favour. They even magnified this 'diversity' and insisted more and more on it.[9] To provide historical justifications to these facts, the task of writing Indian history was undertaken by the colonial administrators.

Consequently, the opposing Anglo-Indian group proceeded to show that not only were all Indian racial and religious groups separate from one another, but there was a chronic antagonism between Hindus and Muslims. Sir Henry James traced the sequence of Hindu-Muslim friction to the

9. See K.K. Aziz, *Britain and Muslim India*, (London, 1963), pp. 33-35 and 4.
Dr. Aziz writes, The insistence on Indian diversity was in fact a reaction to the two opposing myths, those of Indian unity and divide and rule. . . . Professor Seeley threw his weight on the side of disunity and told his students at Oxford that the name India ought not to be classified with such names as England and France, but with such as Europe, which marked a group of nationalities. He warned that from the moment the feeling of a common nationality began to exist in India even if only feebly, the British empire would cease to exist. Later Lord Bryce was to join forces with Seeley and to underline the vital role of religion in the East, where it replaced national feeling.

aggressiveness and recently revived religious activity of the Hindus.[10] Beck also found the Hindu of the new school aggressive and revengeful and 'vigilant and pitiless' in his efforts to ruin the Muslim. Ward attributed the antagonisms to four causes; past rule of the Muslims, 'arrogance and pride of place' of the Hindus, establishment of the Congress and the Home Rule institution introduced by Lord Ripon.[11]

The All Indian National Congress was founded in 1885 by a retired British administrator A.O. Hume to use it as a 'safety-valve,' to keep information of the day to day political developments of the Indian people, to retard it and to check its growth. One may find an easy connection between the establishment of the Congress and the eruptions of communal riots as a recurrent and regular feature of life since 1890. One may ask again that the Hindu and the Muslim masses fought together against imperial exploitation even in the absence of modern political consciousness and before the formation of any political organisations. And this unity could not reappear again till 1947 and after, even after the efforts made by the political leaders to encourage mutual forbearance and unity. The Khilafat question that brought Hindu-Muslim pact at the upper level of the society had nothing to do with native problems. It was only a marriage of convenience between the elites of the two communities on an international issue. Therefore, this effort of unity was destined to end in disaster.

Attempts were made by several intelligentsia and the nationalist leaders to evolve a synthesis of Hindu-Muslim

10. H.E.M. James, 'Reflections on the 'Vay Home' in *National Review*, November 1893, pp. 342-346.
Also see, K.K. Aziz, op.cit , pp. 32-33

11. Ibid. Dr Aziz writes, "A glance at the record of Hindu-Muslim riots between 1870 and 1893 could have convinced every one of the seriousness of the situation. One cause of this trouble might have been that during the first four years of this period the Hindu and Muslim religious festivals coincided; but it was not a mere coincidence that the Congress was founded in 1885.

culture through the preaching of the gospel of unity at the mass level. The people were appealed to bury their differences on the religious line because communal violence appeared to them as the 'ill-will arising out of the ignorance of true religion.' And it could be solved by merely bringing the 'unity of hearts' beween the members of the two communities.[12] Far from it, communal problem was quite over non-religious issue and more often the communal riots did take place on secular issue i.e. conflicts over lands, resentment against Zamindari oppression, against moneylending, to seek jobs in the Government services and even to achieve High Court judgeship. But more often religious garb to the struggle of purely class character was given by the vested interests.

Another major strand regarding communal violence is that it is basically a middle class problem. Contrary to the imperialist insistence on divisions in the Indian society, a large band of nationalist leaders in reaction to it maintained that 'masses were quite free from communal disharmony.' It were the upper class people who fought for their own economic and political ends, and the masses were exploited in the name of religion. The common people fought only because their leaders fought.[13] This view received currency in reaction to the view that 'division has always pervaded Indian society and Hindu-Muslim problem was basically an inevitable product of the Indian historical development.' It was propounded by the colonial writers and their Indian counterparts.

The proposition that though there was acute tension in the society on communal lines, there was still some element of communal harmony at the mass level, is even supported by the progressive school of historians. Dr. V.C.P. Choudhary advances the same view and to him communal tension is basic to the colonial administration.[14] It has already been said that

12. This view was supported by Mahatma Gandhi who was basically a religious man. It has been pointed out elsewhere.
13. *The Behar Herald*, 7th June 1924.
14. Dr. V.C.P. Choudhary, *Secularism versus Communalism* (Patna, 1977), p 21.

communal tension arose out of frustration of one class against the other. 'This frustration, a sense of social deprivation and a constant fear of loss of identity and status often created an atmosphere of violence and brutality which when triggered off by religious issue led to communal riots.'[15] The frustration existed not only at the upper level of the society but the poor peasants and workers too shared the same destiny. To the leaders during the national movement, communal conflict was the conflict of the upper section against shrinking national resources. Even Gandhiji believed that 'if our leaders join hands, the problem could have been solved.'[16]

It is therefore an elitist view regarding the understanding of communal problem and seeking solutions to tackle it. Needless to say that communal problem was a non-religious problem and had wider links with the masses. The acute social tension prevailed at the mass level, though necessarily on class basis which found its expression in caste and communal violence.

One the other hand, Hindu communalists' view regarding the solution of the problem was 'strengthen our own community' and thus force the others to join the banner. The same view has been reflected in the speech delivered by Bhai Parmanand, a recognised Hindu Mahasabha leader. He spoke, "Hindu-Muslim unity is of course a nice thing but we should understand it once that the more the Congress lays stress on Hindu-Muslim unity as a condition precedent to 'swarajya' the greater will be the chances of Musalmans going over to the side of the British Government and widening of the gulf between the two communities. The only possible way of unity is to unify and strengthen the Hindus in such a way as to make it worthwhile for the Musalmans to unite with

15. Bipan Chandra, op.cit., p. 36.
16. Ibid., p. 48.

'The nationalist leaders' efforts to solve the communal problem mainly took the form of negotiating at the top with the recognised communal leaders.'

the Hindus."[17] The communalists' attempt of bringing peace through it was a major challenge to the top nationalist leaders who endeavoured to bring it through constitutional means.

Communal question is a highly complex phenomenon like any other social phenomenon. There are aspects which are very obvious and often talked about and commented on and there are aspects which are very subtle and often we are not conscious about them. The former are mostly of religious and political nature, whereas the latter entail social attitudes and activities of landlords, bureaucrats, imperialists and bourgeoisie.

Social attitudes are again very complex in their origin and structure and manifest themselves in the form of prejudices and stereotypes about the other communities, castes and groups. It should also be remembered that these attitudes and stereotypes are structured over a long period of time, and once formed, keep lingering on often unconsciously in our mind, colouring our perceptions and behavioural pattern. These attitudes manifest themselves in many diverse forms and often are not recognisable easily. These subtler forms of caste and communal attitudes may not directly cause a caste or communal riots but do in one or the other way contribute to aggravation of the situation.

Another far more important aspect of this problem is economic. It shall be discussed in Chapter I that 'every society slave owning, feudal or capitalist has a characteristic structure which enables certain sections of it to appropriate the greater part of material wealth or other privileges by depriving other sections of their legitimate share. All such societies are divided apart from class divisions along lines of caste and creed.' Those who seek to appropriate the greater part of the 'national cake' use caste and creed idioms to make it acceptable to those whom they like to dispossess. Thus

17. *The Behar Herald*, 20th April 1935.
A conference regarding Hindu-Muslim Unity held in Darjeeling.

socio-economic issues, projected in religious idiom, acquire an emotional base around which communal riots occur. However, for the masses, the linkage of socio-economic category with the religious one remains rather obscure and the religious category comes to dominate their imagination. The ruling classes, the bourgeoisie and the bureaucracy in a crisis-ridden economy always try to promote ethnic and communal politics to confuse and criss-cross with class conflicts.

How the economic grievances of the masses remain obscure may be sought in the socio-religious demands of the people. The movement against cow slaughter was largely supported by the Hindu masses though more often initiatives were taken by the landlords, the bureaucrats and other vested interests groups. On the other hand, insistence on cow slaughter by the large population of the Muslim masses was also not without reason. It should not be treated merely as a 'reaction' against the Hindus' voice of banning cow slaughter. Far from it, the slaughter of animal was more a necessity for the poorer section of the Muslim population than religiosity, that it provided cheaper food to them, and that the lower class Muslims were exclusively engaged in the leather trade. It is significant to note that during those days and even today, the high class Muslim hardly favour slaughter.

These economic grievances of the people were later on exploited by the Hindu and the Muslim communalists who provided religious garb to it. Therefore, the protection of cattle became the sole objectives of the Hindus and the sacrifice of it became Islamic for the Muslims. In this way, the whole situation appeared to be the religious and the real issue got obscured.

One may ask too, if the issues behind Hindu-Muslim tension did lie in socio-economic problems, why the temples and the mosques were attacked when the actual trouble did erupt? The answer would be twofold: firstly it was done to secure mass support by appealing to the religion of the masses and secondly to use it as a hideouts and storage of arms to fight. The attack by the people of one community against other was directed towards the religious places partly to win the hearts of their community men and partly to destroy the weapons of the rival or to seize them. One may take note of the Akali Movement in this connection.

On the basis of above mentioned theories regarding communal conflict, it has been attempted promptly to build up an adequate theory of communal violence in India. It is because, in lack of proper concept of the problem, efforts to solve it is certainly like groping in the dark.

1

Communal Riots: Nature and Concept

Number of empirical studies have been carried out on communal riots by several historians and sociologists differing in their basic concepts. Still it is quite relevant today to discuss and make a clear understanding of this complex phenomenon. The significance of the communal riots may be traced back to the medieval period of history but communalism is of course a modern creation, one of the by-products of the colonial economy. At surface, communalism and communal riots may appear to be the same thing but both are distinguishable. The distinction was first brought out by W.C. Smith and K.B. Krishna.[1]

Communalism breeds communal politics whereas communal riots are the clear manifestations of communal tension. Communal tension is spasmodic and usually 'directly involves the lower classes only.' During the period when, and in the area where, communal tension prevails, all mutual relations between the followers of different religions are snapped following the arousal of religious and communal passions

1. K.B. Krishna, *The Problem of Minorities*, (London, 1939), pp. 277-79.
Also see, W.C. Smith, *Modern Islam in India*, (Lahore, 1963), pp. 194-97.

through vicious propaganda, oral as well as written, inflammatory accusations, and wild rumours often involving some religious issues such as 'Cow-killing' or 'music before mosque.'[2] An atmosphere and climate of excitement and frenzy are generated and often actual violence also takes place. The communal riot is a typical example of communal tension. The participants and the victims of a communal riot—though not necessarily its instigators, are usually the urban poor, lumpen and goonda elements, though in some cases peasants are also involved. There are seldom any physical participation by the middle and upper classes, though they often lend material and moral support to the lumpen and goonda participants.[3]

Communal politics, on the other hand, are long term, persistent and continuous. They involve, in the main, the middle classes, landlords and bureaucratic elements.[4] They represent communal ideology in the political form and find expression in the political field. On the personal plane, friendly relations could prevail among the communal politicians as well as their upper class and middle class supporters. In the riots, in the city the poor Hindus and Muslims have their heads split and the upper class section of Hindus and Muslims live in a friendly manner side by side. They dine and drink with each other.[5]

Another significant characteristic of communal riots is that it had a tendency to force even basically secular persons to think temporarily in communal terms to provide for the safety of person and property and thus to generate a vicious circle. In this way, communal riots have a psychological explanation too. Jawahar Lal Nehru was greatly affected by

2. Bipan Chandra, *Communalism in Modern India*, (New Delhi, 1984), p. 4.
3. The idea has been formed after indepth study of communal violence during the period under study. In Chapter V it has been dicussed in detail.
4. Bipan Chandra, op. cit., p. 4.
5. Tufail Ahmed Mangalori, *Mussalman Ka Roshan Mustaqbil*, (Delhi, 1945), pp. 419-20.

the Calcutta tragedy of 1946 and the way it affected the psychology of the people. He remarked, "Even those who never thought in terms of communalism are becoming communal minded. The madness has spread."[6] Moreover, a communal riot left a certain emotional residue or lagacy which could be used later by the communal ideologue or communal politicians. It is to be noted that a direct relationship between communal riots and politics was established for the first time as late as 1946 when the Muslim League gave the direct action call on 6th August.[7]

In this work our main concern will be communal tension, for communal riots are not the main form or content of communalism. They are in the main, its reflections, its active episodic expression, its bitter and virulent manifestation and consequence and one of the instruments and agencies for its spread. The communal riot is an aspect of social pathology, and its causation lay either in the prevalence of a communal atmosphere generated by communal politics and communal ideology involving religious feelings alone or combined with some particular local interests.

Having brought a distinction between these two terms, it would be necessary to take into account the dynamics of economic development and social change in order to develop an adequate theory of communal violence. Any theory which tends to ignore this aspect cannot adequately explain the true nature of communal or caste violence in modern India. But unfortunately most of the explanations put forward still tend to put more than necessary emphasis on the British imperialist policy on the one hand, and the role of history, especially of the Muslim period, on the other.[8] One may go one step further and maintain that in the face of socio-economic changes the role of different political parties, even though

6. S.M. Chand, *National Leaders on Communalism*, (Jaipur, 1985), p. 63.
7. Bipan Chandra, op. cit., p. 6.
8. Ashghar Ali Engineer, *On Developing Theory of Communal Riots* (Bombay, 1984), p. 2.

claiming to be ideologically secular, will also have to be thoroughly examined in promoting communalism which ultimately results at one stage or the other in outbreak of communal violence.

Now efforts would be made to elaborate some of these points and throw light on some of the characteristics of the theory of communal violence which can be said to have greater applicability today. To begin with, it would be emphasised that in any communal riot there involved are micro as well as macro-level factors."[9] Whereas macro-level factors are ideologically oriented, the micro-level factors tend to be local issue oriented. However, it is important to note that both the macro and micro level factors are integrally connected with the socio-economic developments taking place in the country. In other words the whole problem should be viewed in the perspective of the dynamics of social change and development. A social scientist has to take the changes in the base seriously to grapple with the changes taking place in the super-structure, though without trying to establish one to one relation between the two, as often observed.

In order to understand the nature of communal violence in Modern India one also has to understand the role of various classes, social organisations, political parties—communal as well as secular—and the aspirations of the elites of the communities involved in the conflict. It should also be kept in view that contrary to the impression carried out by the people in general religion is not the root cause of the communal conflict; it is rather a powerful instrument in the hands of those interests which seek to play their games through it. It is wrong to make it 'cause celebre' as it is often sought to be done by the vested interests, political as well as economic, who want to hide the real intentions from the masses. It should, however, be made clear that communal riots are not 'merely religious conflicts but are the techniques and weapons adopted by the vested interests in their class

9. A.A. Engineer, op. cit., p. 2.

struggle against the poor.'[10] Such appears to be the real design and class character of the most of the communal riots. This helped both landlords and Britishers to 'divide and rule.' This theory is more relevant even today. Mr. Rajiv Gandhi, in his long delivered lecture in the Rajya Sabha asked the opposition parties 'to make a firm commitment that they would *not use* communalism as a political weapon,' and he loudly lamented that 'the opposition had a vested interest seeing that the poor remained poor.'[11]

Many good intentioned secularists and nationalists too, often make this mistake of holding religion as the main culprit in this matter. It is, to say the least, rather unsociological approach to communal violence —the reasons for which lay in sectarian doctrinaire differences—the communal violence—the reasons for which lay in the conflict over controlling political power and economic resources between the elites of the two communities.[12] Even the nationalist leader like Mahatma Gandhi was not clear in his mind about the real character of the communal violence. However, his tireless endeavours to solve the problem in the course of the national movement proved less worthy because it could not have been solved merely by bringing the 'unity of hearts' between the two communities. As Gandhiji remarked:

> "For me the only question for immediate solution before the country is the Hindu-Muslim question... . I see no way of achieving anything in this afflicted country without a lasting heart unity between Hindus and Muslims of India."[13]

10. Dr. V.C.P. Chcudhary, *Secularism Versus Communalism*, (Patna, 1977), p. 23.
11. *The Indian Nation*, dated 6th March 1986. The news published entitled "PM seeks opposition vow not to use communalism as tool".
12. A.A. Engineer, *op. cit.*, p. 2.
13. *The Behar Herald* (English, Patna) dated 7th June 1924. Extract from the published long speech delivered by Mahatma Gandhi dealing with Hindu-Muslim tension in India.

But Gandhiji was not unaware of the involvement of the vested interests in often igniting communal tension. He further says, '... I think that masses do not want to fight if the leaders do not.' If is precisely for this reason that communalism is borne of secular issues and communal parties led by, or communalism promoted by secular leaders. It is not therefore surprising that the Muslim League in pre-partition period was led by M.A. Jinnah, a thoroughly westernized, even modernised Muslim and the chief ideologue of Hindu Mahasabha V.D. Savarkar had a modern outlook and stood for reforming Hinduism from within. Neither Hindu Mahasabha nor Muslim League was led by a 'Mullah' or 'Shankaracharya'. Communalism is all about secular issues without involving any religious sectarian issues.[14] So the instrumentality of religion should not cause us any confusion as to the real nature of communal violence. Sometimes it may appear that religion is the bone of contention between the two communities because riots originate out of some religious issues like cow sacrifices and music before mosque and often attacks are made on the temples and the mosques.[15] Religious issues are brought only to exploit the sentiment of the masses and religious institutions are often attacked by the rioters of any party because they are the repository of arms.

Now we first propose to deal with the macro factors involved in promoting and accentuating communal violence. The most important aspect of macro level theory is the class character of the society on the one hand, and underdevelopment of economy and scarcity of resources, on the other. The underdevelopment of economy often results in uneven development of economy, both community as well as regionwise and this uneven development throws up the problem of communal o, regional identity. What we are witnessing in Assam and Punjab today is a similar phenomenon.

14. A.A. Engineer, op. cit., p. 3.
15. Gopal Krishna's article 'Socio-economic roots of Punjab crisis,' in *Economic and Political Weekly*, Jan. 12, 1985, Vol. XX, No. 2, pp 61-63.

The uneven development community-wise leads to a situation where intercommunal cohesive class structure does not develop whether it be the development of capitalist class or proletarian class structure. Thus the upper classes of the less developed community feel a strong sense of rivalry vis-a-vis their counterpart in the other community which has gained upper hand. And, in such a situation, in order to win the support of the masses of one community, the grievances are formulated, not in one's class terms but in terms of those of one community. This can best be done by adding a few religio-cultural demands to the down-to-earth economic demands on one hand, and by mythologising the community's past on the other. Thus we see that the communalists among both the communities have often glorified their respective past and project it as a 'golden period' free of inter-class or inter-ethnic conflict. The mythologising and romanticising one's community's past serves as a very powerful instrument for mobilizing the masses for realising class aspirations. Such an instrument proves far more powerful in a socially backward society like India.[16]

In a backward and communally divided society like India, it becomes very difficult to develop class solidarity across communal lines, especially in case of working class which, ironically, happen to be the main victim of communal violence.[17] In this case mythologised version of history as well as other powerful myths cleverly manipulated by the exploiting classes have far greater mobilising potentiality than

16. A.A. Engineer, op. cit , p. 4.
Also see, Bipan Chandra's article 'Communalism and the Historians of Modern India' in *Communalism and the Writings of Indian History* (Delhi, 1981), p. 47.

17. It is obvious from the survey of communal riots (1890-1948) that the lower sections of the society and economically backward like Dusadh, Chamar, Dom, Tantis, Momins, Jullahas etc. participated in the actual fighting.

their own class interests. It is particularly true of urban petty bourgeois classes.[18]

For developing theory of communal coflict there is another problem at the mass level to be taken into consideration. It is integrally connected with the dynamics of social change in the country. Socio-economic changes, especially in a tradition bound society, bring about deep sense of insecurity among those strata of society which are adversely affected by it. Working as well as petty-bourgeois classes are usually the worse affected in such a situation. They are tradition-prone and the 'sense of insecurity' accompanying socio-economic change reinforces this tendency among them.[19] Thus they provide fertile ground for religious, revivalist movements. On the contrary, sense of insecurity generated by such socio-economic changes for a sizeable section of the society increases appeal of religion by providing solace and reducing psychological tensions involved.

These psychological tensions are also very complex and manifest themselves in the form of prejudices and stereotypes about the other communities, castes and groups.[20] It should also be remembered that these attitudes and stereotypes are structured over a long period of time, and once formed, keep lingering on often unconsciously in our minds colouring our perceptions and behavioural pattern. These attitudes manifest

18. Bipan Chandra's article 'Communalism and the Historians of Modern India' in *Communalism and the Writings of Indian History*, (New Delhi, 1981), p. 48.

    He wriies, "Communalism among a section of the Indian people, especially among the historians, spread mainly because of its ability to serve as 'vicarious' and 'backdoor' nationalism. Communalism enabled them to feel nationalistic without opposing imperialism, the foreign power that was then ruling and appressing the Indian people. It enabled them to combine personal safety with nationalist sentiments."

19. A.A. Engineer, op. cit., p.

20. A.A. Engineer's article, 'Theory of communal riots; subtler aspects in *Mainstream*, May 19, 1984, Vol. XXII, No. .8, p. 15.

themselves in most diverse forms and often are not recognisable easily. These subtler forms of caste and communal attitudes may not directly cause a caste or communal riot but do in one or the other way contribute to aggravation of the situation.[21]

In respect of these subtler belief and attitudes the most commonly held one is that a Muslim somehow happens to be always aggressor and has a strong sense of solidarity with other Muslims, while others, especially the Hindus, are non-violent, more tolerant and totally lacking any sense of solidarity with their co-religionists.[22] Needless to say, neither the Muslims are always aggressive nor the Hindus always tolerant and non-violent. Girilal Jain, editor, "The Times of India" for example writes in one of his articles that "the community sense among Muslims is stronger than among bindus."[23] But it does not stand scrutiny of empirical reality. Muslims are as much divided as any other religious community along class lines alone as well as ethnic, cultural and caste and sectarian lines.[24] In such a situation it would be a prejudiced assumption to maintain that a particular community would be non-violent and tolerant compared to other community only because these are religious ideals. It is to fly in the face of empirical facts to maintain that a community's socio-political conduct is primarily governed by its religious ideals, whatever the ideals might be. Even past

21. Ibid.
22. The idea is based on the interviews taken from some of the Hindus. Most of them believed that the Muslims are anti-nationalist, traitors and more cohesive than them. But at the same time one finds ready answer to it when most of the Muslims think of Hindus as a solid group having unbreakable unity among themselves. If one talks to an individual belonging to particular caste, he will remark that everywhere unity exists along caste lines except theirs. The reply of the persons belonging to other caste will follow the same pattern. They themselves will show disunited in comparison to others.
23. *The Times of India*, dated 17th February 1984.
24. A.A. Engineer, 'Theory of Communal Riots' in *Mainstream*, May 19, 1984.

history does not seem to support the claim that Hindus had always been tolerant and non-violent and Muslims the aggressor.

Thus Genes and Silveira maintain in their book 'The long Road of Time,'

> "The excesses committed by the Hindu fighting men in Ahmadnagar roused widespread feelings of anger and indignation throughout the Deccan sultanates...Mosques had been razed to the ground or used as stables, villages have been destroyed, the people have been massacred."[25]

The myths and half truths thus imparted to the children in schools at a tender age becomes an important part of their mental baggage which they are not rid throughout their lives. All this helps in forming and crystallising certain stereotypes in one community towards other community. One community develops hatred towards the other and the other a strong feeling of guilt. However, even those who become secular in their ideology and give up their communal attitudes consciously, carry in the depth of their sub-conscious hangover of these attitudes and beliefs which are manifested in the most subtle forms.[26]

Also the stereotypes that the Muslims are in general polygamous and tend to produce a large number of children irrespective of their social and class status is also widely prevalent. It is prevalent about Muslims that they do not practise family planning and strongly resist any attempt in

25. A.A. Engineer, op. cit., p. 35.
26. Ibid., pp. 35-37.

N.C Saxena in his article 'Secularism and our next books' writes, "History as it is taught in schools in the form of History or Hindi text books, is full of sectarian and communal biars." The Hindu and Muslim communalists thus project Indian history in terms of an unrelieved struggle between the two religious communities in India.

that direction.[27] In fact the socio-religious organisations play their decisive role in structuring such stereotypes among the people who are basically illiterate. The '*Patit Pawan*' and the '*Vishwa Hindu Parishad*' in Maharashtra had launched a door-to-door campaign that as Muslims are polygamous, and they are multiplying very fast and within the coming twenty years they will outnumber the Hindus and that India would become a Muslim majority state. Madan Mohan Malviya once reflected the same belief in his speech that 'it is really a sorry affair that birth rate among the Hindus have decreased and death rate increased...cowardice has taken place of bravery.'[28]

It needs some discussion here. The acceptance or rejection of family planning very much depends on one's socio-economic status. Those people either Hindu or Muslim belong to middle class and live in towns and cities, readily take to restricting their children whereas those who belong to artisan and working classes do not do so as readily and tend to produce more children. Thus M.E Khan in his research paper 'Knowledge, Attitude and Practice of Family Planning among Muslims in an urban setting' concludes, "Among the Muslims it is their comparative backwardness which is the real cause of motivation for family planning rather than doctrinal consideration of their religion.... In third world

27. A pamphlet distributed in Bombay during 'Ekatmata Yagna' in which the Muslims have been shown with the slogan—"Ham Panch Aur Hamare Pachehis," dated Nov. 16, 1983. Department of family welfare, Government of India, also issued such inflammatory information without any consideration for its consequences. May we remind them that the national policy is to promote secularism, not fears of religious groups organised on communal lines?
See Pramod Kumar & Bhupinder Yadav's article 'Communalism and National Integration' in *The Mainstream*, dated 23 Feb. 1985, Vol. XXIII., No. 26, p. 25.

28. *The Behar Herald* , January 6, 1923.
At the same time Mr. Rajendra Prasad talks of 'Hindu rights'. He says, "The Hindus would realise the supreme necessity of unity among communities and that they would give serious consideration of an All-India Hindu Paksha Society for the protection of Hindu rights." See Ibid.

countries people multiply much faster because they are economically backward."

Thus the image of Muslim as fanatic, oppressive, resistant to any change and inherently communal has persisted too long and there has been hardly any attempt to study Muslim attitudes empirically with scientific rigour. Many a time such attitudes collectively held among the Hindus easily lend themselves to creating a communal atmosphere which ultimately leads to rioting and violence. These are subtler aspects of communal tension and a theory cannot ignore them as they have dangerous potentials. However, it does not mean that Muslims do not entertain wrong attitudes and stereotypes towards Hindus. Any theory on this problem cannot ignore this aspect too.

In the middle and lower middle classes, the problem of attitudes and stereotypes assumes serious proportions. These classes are also articulating classes and matter very much in formulating public opinion.[29] The attitudes and stereotpes, conscious or otherwise, therefore matter very much among these classes of both communities. The middle classes were, during the freedom struggle, at the very centre of conflict and attitudes formed during these periods, kept on colouring our mentality in hostility to the other community. The Muslim League and the Hindu Mahasabha for their political expediency during the pre-independence period, often aroused religious hostility of the middle and lower middle classes of

29. See, Pramod Kumar & Bhupinder Yadav's article, op. cit., p. 27 'It is worthy of note that the educated urban elite, aided and abetted by powerful vested interests, which articulates and leads communal movememts not only because it has capacity to articulate but also because of its percepation that its interests are harmed. The educated urban elite, otherwise quite secular, and often posing itself to be secular, uses religious or similar other parochial sentiments for advancing or protecting its own interests. Sacred is thus used for secular ends. It is this specific combination that gives rise to the phenomenon of communal politics and violence.

their respective community.[30] This stereotype, developed as it did during the period of intense conflict, has struck and often unconsciously influences inter-communal behaviour between Hindus and Muslims.

A very common stereotype developed in independent India among the Muslim community consequent to the creation of Pakistan. North Indian Muslims began to suffer from what can be described as 'Pakistan complex.' This complex finds expressions in various ways which is used by Hindu communal organisations for arousing hostility towards them.[31] A common place form of this 'complex' is the reaction of Muslims during Cricket or Hockey matches with Pakistan. Regrettably many Muslims manifest pro-Pakistani feelings during such matches. Many a communal riot has taken place in independent India using it as a pretext.

The perception of one community about the other does not depend directly on objective reality but on the psychological complex of socio-religio-political prejudices. These attitudes and complexes in the event of a fast deteriorating communal situation, make people more amenable to believe certain rumours, and these rumours play havoc. One can cite numerous instances of the role played by rumours in communal riots. Such instances may be seen in other chapters.

Now it becomes all the more necessary to explore; why do communal riots occur? What purpose, if any, do they serve? What conditions aggravate communal conflict? These

30. At several places religious susceptibilities were aroused by the communal leaders of the two communities. 'Religion in danger became the popular slogan of the Muslim communalism and on the other hand Hindus were taught to fight and die for the protection of 'Hinduism' and Hindu rights.

See 'Vir Sawarkar's warning to Bihari Hindus,' an extract from the speech published in *The Aryavarta* (Hindi, daily) dated 28th June 1947.

31. A.A. Engineer, op. cit., p. 9.

are extremely difficult questions to which Indian social science has not addressed itself with the requisite degree of seriousness. The Indian discussions of this subject have been simplistic and moralistic. The simplistic explanation of communal conflict in pre-independence period was in terms of the imperialist conspiracy to 'divide and rule.' In this connection one may quote Francis Robinson who remarked that:

> Indian nationalists found the arguement particularly attractive and accuse their imperial rulers of having broken an evolving synthesis of Hindu-Muslim culture.'[32]

This is now replaced by a Marxist equivalent i.e., it is the capitalist conspiracy. At a more sophisticated level communal conflict is sought to be explained by Marxists as an inevitable consequence of the contemporary capitalist order.[33]

Among the non-Marxists there are at least three strands:

The first one could be said to represent the view that communal conflict is in truth a result of mutual ignorance, only if the Hindus and the Muslims knew that all religious were 'fundamentally' one and if they approached each other with good will there will be no conflict. This is a Hindu religiously oriented view which characterised the reflections of the late Bhagwandas.[34]

The second strand is represented by the power theory of communal conflict. This holds that given the strongly developed communal identities Hindus and Muslims were bound to conflict over the question of who is to control the

32. Francis Robinson, *Separatism among Indian Muslims*, (Delhi, 1975), p. 21.
33. A.A. Engineer's article, 'Communal Riots; subtler aspects' in *Mainstream* dated August 20, 1983.
34. N.G. Barrier, (ed) "Roots of Communal Politics", (Delhi, 1976), p. 102.

state because control over state is of primary importance in preserving the culture and identity of the community and promoting the welfare of its members. This theory lay at the Muslim League's demand for partition, which Jinnah believed to be in the interest not only of the Muslims but also of the Hindus.

The third strand takes communal conflict in the post-independence context, to be a part of the competitive political process, except that it ought to be rendered free of violence. The argument here is that democracy flourishes when there is group competition, and that in India we have a group structure primarily consisting of religious communities and competition between them as well as the constraints they might succeed in imposing upon the state are likely to strengthen democracy. This is he view advanced by Humayun Kabir.[35]

Lastly there is the Hindu communalist theory that views minorities as enemy of the nation and communal violence as deliberate acts intended to humiliate and injure the Hindus. Its counterpart is the Muslim communalist theory which considers communal violence as well organised, pre-planned Hindu attacks designed to terrorise the Muslims, to depress them, to drive them out of their own areas, to reduce them to second class citizens.[36]

35. Humayun Kabir, *Minorities in a Democracy*, (Calcutta, 1968), p. 59.
36. On the same issue, a corresponding hatred is seen in writings of communal Muslims. For example, F.K. Khan Darrani in *The Meaning of Pakistan* (Lahore, 1944) had the following observations on the life style and greed of the members of Hindu religious group:
"The Hindus live to earn and hoard, while the Muslim earns to live and spend. The Hindu's inordinate love of money is a most amazing phenomenon. The food he eats is wretched. . . . To the Hindus it has given a peculiar character, a peculiar cast of mind, a habit of thought which we Muslims of Northern India just do not understand, and the same is more or less true of the Muslims of other parts of India. . . . Jews are but small minorities in western lands, whereas our Jews are the overwhelming majority."

On these 'theories' the question why do the communal riots occur can be answered as follows:

The Marxist answer would be (a) it is a conspiracy of the capitalist class to divide the working class and to check their unity and growing consciousness against oppression, or (b) it is an incipient fascism of an unsteady, underdeveloped capitalism, or (c) uneven access to economic resources leads to violence. The religious answer is that riots take place due to mutual ignorance of true religion and ill-will borne out of that ignorance. The power theory answer will be that violence occurs because the communities have been denied power and the democratic theory's answer will be that violence occurs because democratic rights of groups are in some important ways restricted and the communalists, answer is that violence is a part of a well designed conspiracy to achieve dominance.

From these formulations emerge recommendations for policies designed to control and eventually abolish communal violence. Experience has taught us that communal violence is an expression of frustration in one context but 'it is an instrument of power in another, more power to the communities, or greater scope for communal self-expression in a democracy, can aggravate communal conflict and ultimately disrupt the state.'[37]

Here brief explanation of the different theories regarding communal violence is sought to be necessary to develop on adequate theory of it. Communal conflict does not seem to originate out of the ignorance of true religion but in the struggle for autonomy on the part of one or more groups and there is an inescapable conflict between their drive for autonomy and the cohesion of the state in multi-religious society. 'Politicisation of religion, conditions of extreme scarcity, and particularly divisive style of politics aggravate the problem which appears to be basic to heterogeneous societies. The

37. Prabha Dixit, *Communalism—A struggle for power*, (New Delhi, 1974), p. 206.

institutional structure for overcoming the pluralist impediments to integration is in place in India. It is well conceived.'[38]

Religion must not be treated as the sole culprit in communal tension nor can it be mistaken as the villian of peace. Mr. Jay Prakash Narain, a great socialist leader had clear view of the nature of communal tension and the politics behind it. He loudly lamented,

> "It is however not the fault of religion that it allows itself to be exploited by communalists. The arch culprit is the politics, followed clearly by economics. Behind communal riots religion had never been the real issue but there is no doubt that every such riot adds to the popularity of one or other communal party or group; and strengthens the economic interests in the field of trade, manufacture, moneylending etc. of one religious community or other."[39]

If one looks at this problem in the Marxist perspective, one finds a ready answer to it in this way. Since both the Hindus and the Muslims are divided into two sections, the exploiters and the exploited or haves and haves not. There are no common political and economic interests of all Hindus

38. Gopal Krishna's article 'Communal violence in India' in *Economic and Political Weekly*, Jan. 12, 1985, Vol. XX, No. 2, p.63.
39. Extract from the speech of J.P. Narain addressed to the 'Second National Connection against Communalism' in Delhi, 1968 in S.M. Chand, *National Leaders on Communalism*, (Jaipur, 1985). Also see, W.C Smith, *Modern Islam in India*, (Lahore, 197?), p. 227.
W C. Smith has rightly pointed out, "Religion is used as an instrument to provide justification for acts which are otherwise inhuman and undesirable. Further, history has many times shown that religion is ready to excuse atrocities. . . . Moreover, once a conflict has started for economic or other reasons and then assumes a communalist guise, it tends to expand to include innocent correligionists of the real enemies. Also, it tends to colour the thinking of the persons involved for all their other issues."

as such and all Muslims as such. British colonialism was nursed by Indian capitalism, the growth and development of which was a joint responsibility of both the communities. 'And the struggle between the exploiters and the exploited, in fact was nothing but a class struggle, was given a communal coating.'[40]

Communal tensions are at bottom class struggles. 'They take a communal shape because of the general background of the country, because the classes belong to various faiths. Religion is invoked to conceal their secular interests.'[41] An important thinker of Modern India C.G. Shah also remarked in the same vein. He says,

> "Under the pressure of communal propaganda the masses are unable to locate the real causes of their exploitation, oppression and suffering and imagine a fictitious communal source of their origin."[42]

We may also note that mobilisation of the peasantry around religious symbols, slogans and idealogies in their struggle against agrarian oppression is a common occurrence in pre-modern societies. But often a communal colour is given to the social conflict not by the participants, but by the observer, the official, the politicians, the journalists and in the end historians in their vested class interests.[43] Tanika Sarkar's conclusion is that "what were fundamentally agrarian jacqueries or the fury of the urban poor against a social system reinforced by an alien imperialism turned into communal fighting due to imperfect politicisation."[44]

40. K.K. Wadhwa, *Minorities' Safeguards in India*, (Delhi, 1975), p. 27.
41. K.B. Krishna, op.cit., p. 272.
42. C.G. Shah, *Marxism Gandhism Stalinism*, (Bombay, 1963), p. 185.
43. Bipan Chandra, op.cit , p. 56.
44. Tanika Sarkar's article, 'Communal Riots in Bengal 1930-31' in *Communal and Pan-Islamic Trends in Colonial India*, edited by M. Hasan, (New Delhi, 1981), p. 298.

To sum up, communal riots cannot be understood in isolation from a comprehension of the level of operation of communal ideology. Communal riots as a conjectural outcome of the pervasiveness of communal ideology with communal politics and communal violence. The reports of the various commissions on communal riots illustrate the piecemeal and reductionist approach to enquire into communal riots. The commissions treated communal riots to be equivalent to ordinary crimes committed by individuals and largely dwelled upon them as a law and order problem.[45]

A critical evaluation of the reports of commissions appointed by the Government of India to look into the causes and courses of riots reveal that communal riots have been erupting due to the intolerance of people towards other religion, non-alertness of intelligence and slackness of administrative machinery. The causes for riots are traced to the incidents immediately prior to the conflagration and analysis of riots is lost in the details of the course of events. Hence the whole genesis of riots is seen to lie in religious practices, festivals and processions. The solutions are sought in the formation of peace committees.[46]

Far from it, the elements of protest, ideology, lack of access to normal channels of grievance redressal or the absence of normal methods of interest articulation are relatively significant factors in any particular riot. Besides these characteristics, the notable feature is the spontaneous and unplanned though possibly organised nature of the riots.

45. See long published Oldham's Report on Shahabad riot of 1917 in *Political Special File* No. 112/1917 (B.S.A.), p. 17.

46. S. Gopal (ed), *Jawahar Lal Nehru: Selected Works*, (New Delhi, 1972), Vol. XV, p. 315.
Nehru's statement to the press after Calcutta riots, dated Aug. 26, 1946:
"The most effective method to check these degrading conflicts is the organisation of average citizens for the protection of Mohallas and not the 'peace committees' usually formed during communal riots of the very elements that have caused the trouble."

These riots are organised on the basis of communal ideology. The normal feature is that each incident of communal riot starts with some criminal activity. Further, communalists or instigators who have vested interests, patronise anti-social elements to use them when communal tensions are simmering. It is a fact that spontaneous criminal acts become the immediate cause of communal riots. Generally disturbances are sparked when a person belonging to a particular religious group is assaulted by one belonging to another. Rumour mongering and gossip contribute to aggravating the situation by giving a communal colour to individual acts of crime and violence.

Individual or groups genuinely adhering to communal ideology may use this riff-raff and may actively participate in rioting. These vested interests are involved in severe competition for maximising their profits or enhancing their political power. They mystify the real conflicts and instigate victims of communal ideology to attack misplaced targets. The victims of communal ideology and anti-social elements may not be actually involved in competition but are used as tools by these interests. "The active participants believe that they are the greatest benefactors of their 'community.' They are committed to the visionary idea of creating a new society in which the 'Kafirs' or aliens would have no right to exist." This section is a victim of communal ideology and also the fear psychosis created by communal propaganda. These victims do not necessarily derive their rationalisation from immediate economic or political gains.

The other section of active participants in communal riots may be from among workers lacking class consciousness. They may resort to communal violence in the hope of transforming their wretched living conditions.[47]

47. In most of the communal riots, we may note that large scale loots and dacoities are committed. Shops, granaries, and market complexes become the targets of the rioters. There are several riots of this nature. For example see Bettiah riots of 1927, *Political Special File* No. 216/1927 (B.S.A.).

Accidental beneficiaries of a communal riot belong to sections who are neither victim of communal ideology nor vested interests. Agents of state may be able to white-wash their sins and politicians their misdeeds, small traders can earn a little more profits and landlords get eviction from their premises in a communal riot. These individuals do not belong to any group but may indirectly and accidentally benefit from a riot situation.

Apart from these factors, communal riots were also often the result of the overall fear that the other side would wipe out or dominate us. Petty questions such as cow-killing, music before mosque, throwing of coloured water during the holi festival and cutting down of a 'peepal' tree became the occasions for communal tension because they got tied up with the fears of the people, especially with the problems of petty bourgeois identity, ego and insecurity.[48] They became 'symbols of dominance,' their abandonment or tolerance would show that 'we' were weak and ripe for being dominated. The petty-bourgeois constantly tries to build up its ego.

There is an understandable and perhaps even justified tendency among minorities, whether religious, linguistic or national, to mistrust the majority and to be afraid that their social, religious and cultural interests might suffer because of their weaker numerical position and that the majority might use the force of numbers to injure the minority or absorb it.[49]

From the foregoing discussion it is clear that to develop comprehensive theory of communal conflict one will have to take macro as well as micro factors into account. Among the

48. The fear was basically displayed by the communalists often creating an atmosphere of 'insecurity' among the people. The announcement that 'Hindi is our national language' was projected as an attack on Urdu by the Muslim vested interest. The people were exploited after the arousal of 'false consciousness' among them. See Maulana Hashrat Mohani's statement to *The Aryavarta* dated 7th November 1947.

49. Bipan Chandra, op.cit., p. *139*.

macro factors are countrywide socio-economic changes as a result of following the capitalist path of development, policies pursued by the ruling political parties both of the centre as well as in the states, deliberate attempt to encourage religious fundamentalism by the ruling classes in order to manage the deepening economic crisis through other means etc. The ruling classes as a whole are responsible for encouraging caste and communal identities thus aggravating communal conflict.

At micro-level one must take into account factors like the proportion of Muslim population, nature of economic competition between the two communities, history of communal riots in the area, election politics of local bodies, role of anti-social elements. In any riot both the micro and macro factors play important role, of course varying in degrees from place to place.

At last it might be proposed that caste and communal identities are far more emotionally stronger in this country then the class identity and the ruling classes fully exploit this situation. With the slow process of economic growth the conflict is bound to intensify and in India the ruling c asses can easily divert the conflict from class to caste and communal channel.[50]

50. One may note several social organisations along caste and religicus lines in pre and post independence India. The proliferation of caste and communal organisations get its active support from the ruling party who use it as a weapon against class struggle. The popular resentment of the masses against Zamindari oppression was given caste and communal channel. It has recently been projected in Prakash Jha's film, *Damul* released in 1984.

2

History of Communal Riots-I

The National Picture : Its Changing Horizon

It has been historically approved that the people of this country experienced communal riots as a regular feature of life only after the colonial take over of the Indian economy. It has also been accepted by a number of historians that for such a tension precondition existed in this country and of course, the imperialists in their own interests accentuated and nursed the differences existing in the society.[1] But one should not forget to mention that Hindu-Muslim conflict existed both before the emergence of British power and the introduction of separate electorates in India. Communal identity and division have always pervaded Indian society, though they may have been reinforced in modern times.[2]

Every society slave owning, feudal or capitalist has 'a

1. Several historians as well as the nationalists accept this view and they talk of 'favourable soil.' Pandit Nehru, Rabindra Nath Tagore and R.P. Dutt conform to this group of believers. Chand, *op. cit.*, pp.
2. Bipan Chandra, *Communalism in Modern India*, (Delhi, 1984), p. 4.

characteristic tendency which enables certain section of it to appropriate the greater part of material wealth or other privileges by depriving other sections of the society.... All such societies are divided apart from class divisions along lines of caste and creed.'[3] Since very early in the settlement of the Muslims in India clashes between them and the Hindus may be presumed to have taken place, where the Hindus felt themselves fairly strong and were not wholly cowed down by the military exploits and ruthless power used by the Monarchs. Ibn Batuta, in his long tour during the second half of fourteenth century, has noted that 'there was a colony of about 4,000 Muslims at Manglore ruled over by Ram Deva living in the suburb alongside the town.' He further says that conflicts frequently broken out between them and the towns people, but the sultan makes pace between them on account of his need of merchants.[4]

Recently Mohammad Yasin has observed that during the later Mughal period (1605 to 1748), the relations among the Hindus and Muslims were cordial and characterised by good will, mutual love and toleration, and 'that the fact is borne out by the whole history of Muslim rule in India, where except in the time of later Mughals, there were communal riots on the mass scale which may be ascribed to the mounting reaction of the seventeenth century.[5] It is often admitted by some historians that Emperor Aurangzeb was responsible for increasing Hindu-Muslim tension by trying to Islamise the Mughal Government. But if we go to the root of history, we find that "despite contact, co-operation and mutual influence which reached their height in the time of Akbar who attempted a synthesis of Islam and Hinduism, Muslim and Hindu communities maintained distinct social as well as

3. K. Marx and F. Engels, *Selected Works*, Vol. I (Masco, 1977), fourth edition, p. 449.
4. G.S. Ghurye, *Social Tensions in India*, (Bombay, 1968), p. 304.
5. Mohammad Yasin, *A Social History of Islamic India*. (Lahore, 1958), pp. 50-51.

religious identities."[6] And after Aurangzeb's death in 1707, when Muslim power started disintegrating, Muslims were so alarmed of the growing power of the Hindu Rajas under Maratha leadership that a sufi scholar, Shah Walliullah was inspired to write a letter to Ahmad Shah Abdali to implore India to protect the Muslim position.[7]

In 1713 A.D. according to Khafi Khan, there was what may be called a religious disturbance which took place at Ahmedabad in Gujarat. As this is the first riot properly called.[8] The local official who was a Muslim gave his decision in favour of the Hindus and the latter burnt the holi. The next day, the Muslim gentleman, desiring to give an entertainment in honour of the prophet, slaughtered a cow in front of his house. All the nearby Hindus immediately assembled and attacked the Musalamans found there. In this riot mainly shops were destroyed.[9]

There was a Hindu-Muslim riot in Kashmir in 1719-20, in 1729, in the Vidarbha region of Maharashtra in 1786, occasioned by an attack on the religious processions. The riot that occurred in Kashmir, in origin it was a vendetta of a Muslim gentleman against the Hindus.[10] A little over half a century after the Kashmir affair, in September 1786 in the heart of the country under the nose of the Maratha powers, during what was evidently their hey-day of power and glory, several incidents of this type did take place.

During the first half of the 19th century, there were numerous communal disturbances in Northern India. C.A.

6. Syed Sharifuddin Pirzada, *Foundations of Pakistan*, (Karachi, 1970), Vol. I, Introduction, p. XII.
7. Khaleed B. Sayeed, *Pakistan : A Formative Phase*, (Karachi, 1968), p. 4.
8. G.S. Ghurye, op. cit., p. 306.
   A holiday observed by Hindus by lighting a huge fire and accompanied by shouting of slogans, mostly abusive led to breach of peace.
9. Ibid.
10. G.S. Ghurye, op. cit., p. 306.

Bayly of Cambridge University reports that these occurred at Benaras where Hindus are said to have destroyed fifty mosques.[11] But the description of the riots of Benaras (1809), makes it quite clear that 'it was one of those convulsions which had frequently occurred in the past owing to the religious antagonisms between the Hindu and Musalman section of the population.' Communal feud had been noticed from several other parts,[12] as Koil (1820), Moradabad, Sambhal, Kashipur (1833), Shahjehanpur (1837), Bareilly, Kanpur and Allahabad (1837-52) and among other places. The chief source of conflict at Bareilly, Kanpur and Ahmedabad was the mosque built by Aurangzeb on the site of an old temple. In 1871, the Mohmmad an festival synchronised with the Hindu festival Ram Navmi, and a serious riot was the consequence in Bareilly.[13] Among the causes these clashes was the degrading of the Muslim state functionaries, and the consequent decline of Muslim dominance following the British conquest of the area.[14]

In South India, Hindu-Muslim riots are reported from the middle of the fourteenth century, As W.C. Smith remarks,

> "A Moplah outbreak usually begins with the assassination of a landlord (the bulk of whom are Hindus), the looting of the Hindu shop or defiling of a Hindu temple"[15]

The immediate issue of Hindu-Muslim conflict was the cow slaughter and religious processions. In 1893, major disturbances took place in Azamgarh district over cow-sacrifice. Behind these was the Hindu movement for the protection of the cattle. Though, the cow question has been important at

11. C.A. Bayly, *Rulers, Townsmen and Bazars*, (Cambridge, 1983), p. 335.
12. Ibid.
13. G.S. Ghurye, op. cit., p. 308.
14. C.A. Bayly, op. cit., pp. 335-38.
15. G.S. Ghurye, op. cit., p. 310.

least since the middle ages.[16] Akbar had prohibited cow slaughter in his empire, and the local successor rulers to the Mughal empire had also prohibited it. If we go back to the ancient period of Indian history, the same action regarding cow protection had been taken by Asoka, according to the need of cattle. The cattle for the whole feudal agrarian economy were a great asset to the empire. There was quite lack of any religious affiliation to the cow. But up to these days, the question of cow protection has taken different shape.

The cow protection movement in its new guise owes its origin to the Namdhari Kuka sect of Sikhs around 1870 in Punjab, which later spread to North-West India as well as to UP and Bihar. In 1893, in Mao (Azamgarh) a dispute arose between Hindus and Muslims over the interpretation of the Government order prohibiting all cow sacrifices. The riots that followed, spread over a very wide area, encompassing UP, Bihar, Gujarat and Bombay and claimed out 107 lives.[17] There were 22 riots in Bihar affecting the districts of Saran, Patna, Darbhanga and Gaya.[18] These developments should be viewed as a part of the imperial policy of administering India.

The general revolt of 1857 played a great role in Indian history and in the relation between Hindu and Muslims. According to Sir Alfred Lyall,

> "The English turned friendly on the Muhammadans as upon their real enemies and most dangerous rivals, so that the failure of the revolt was much more disastrous to them than to the Hindus."[19]

16. J.R. Maclane, *Indian Nationalism and the Early Congress*, (Princeton, 1977), pp. 314-21.
17. J.R. Maclane, op. cit., p. 321.
18. *Politicol Policy Proceedings* (1890-95), pp. 25-36 (BSA).
19. A C. Lyall, *Asiatic Studies : Religions and Social*, (London, 1884), edn. 2, pp. 239-40.
Also see, Dr. Padmasha, *Indian National Congress and* Muslims, (New Delhi, (1980), p. 10.

For some decades after the revolt, the Muslims were the villains, Hincus the most pampered subject. After the Indian National Congress began to gather support, the Hindus became suspect and Muslim loyalties were cultivated as a counterpoise.

In the year 1885, Cotton pointed out that significant changes were taking place in India on the line of nationalist agitation. It was the cause of the British fear and that is why Lord Dufferin who came as the viceroy in India in 1884 had frankly admitted:[20]

> "The most potent characteristic of our Indian Cosmos is its division into two mighty communities as distinct from each other as the poles asunder in their religious faiths, their historical antecedents, their social organisation and their natural aptitudes."

It has been noted that since then clever and mischievous propaganda was started on these lines to create hostility between the Hindus and the Muslims.[21] Meanwhile, by 1885, some other factors also had begun working which supported communal feeling. In the first place, the opportunity for Muslim rapproachment with the English came both in Europe and at home. The old anti-party attitude was giving place to a new policy of having sympathy with the Muslim community.

The tendency of Hindu-Muslim tension became apparent from those days. It affected the social, political and economic condition of both the communities. And a competition to get the sympathy of the Government arose between them. Throughout the first three quarters of the 19th century, the Hindus had manifested greater eagerness for the share in administration, while the Muslims stood aloof.[22] Consequently it resulted in the exclusion of the Muslims from

20. A.B. Rajput, *Muslim League : Yesterday and Today*, (Lahore, 1948), p. 14.
21. A.B. Rajput, op. cit., p. 14.
22. Dr. Padmasha, op. cit., p. 15.

having larger share in the loaves and fishes. Thus Hindus and Muslims expressed their direct difference on some socio-economic phenomenon such as cow protection, Hindi-Urdu controversy and assertion of religicus privileges on the occasions of festivals.

But communal disturbances were not a regular feature of life in India in the nineteenth century. In the 20th century the picture has gradually changed. The Government of India in their memorandum to the Indian Statutory Commission mentions riots in East Bengal in 1907, Peshawar in 1910, Ayodhya in 1912, Agra in 1913, Shahabad in 1917 and Katarpur in 1918.[23] The frequency of riots increased during the 1920s and almost every province was affected. There were riots in Malegaon (1921), Multan (1922), Lahore, Amritsar, Saharanpur (1923). The year 1924 saw some major outbreaks in Allahabad, Calcutta, Delhi, Gulbarga, Kohat, Lucknow and Nagpur.[24]

It is necessary to record here that the cause of Bombay riot (1893), 'The worst of the outbreaks of violence ever known in Bombay' was an impression that the Muslim needed special protection and that the European system of administration tended to increase the influence of the Hindus at their expense.[25] On 6th February 1894, the suppressed feelings and tensions of the previous year broke out in the form of serious riot at Yeola in Nasik.[26]

There followed lull for about ten years, though two movements started by the Hindus, one against 'cow slaughter' and the other of public 'Ganapati festival' went on from

23. *Indian Statutory Commission Report* (1930), Vol. IV, Part I, pp. 97-107.
24. The major riots of 1920s are considered in G.R. Thursby, *Hindu-Muslim Relations in British India*, (Leiden, 1975).
25. *Report on the Administration of Bombay Presidency* (1893-94), p. IV.
26. Ibid.

strength to strength. The partition of Bengal made in 1905, the great revival of Kali worship, giving it the form of group performance on the pattern of Ganapati festival and the inauguration of the boycott of foreign goods, initiated the new era of riots in Bengal and soon its repercussions were felt all over the country. It began with serious riots between Hindus and Muslims at several places.

With the onset of the new political era of the Montford scheme and the popularisation of political agitation, riots between Hindus and Muslims one again leapt into the arena, as if to remind the public and the Government that the Hindus and the Muslims had become conscious of the imminent change of power and were intent on having it distributed according to their desires. The period after the introduction of the Montague-Chelmsford reforms stand out in stark contrast with the period which preceded it.[27] During the war years, the Muslim League and the Congress worked together for Constitutional reform, and after the war, Mahatma Gandhi and Ali brothers joined forces to preserve the Khilafat and to gain Swaraj.[28]

After the introduction of the reforms, however, and particularly after the subsidence of the Khilafat and non-co-operation movements, communal unity gave way to communal antagonisms, the fraternization of 1919 seemed an aberration, and many parts of North India were plunged into scenes of bloodshed and strife which were to have no parallel until partition itself.[29]

This new era began with a riot at Malegaon in Nasik district in April 1921. But the rebellion of the Moplahs which started in Malwa in the month of August, threw it into the background. Bangalore followed in the November of 1921.[30]

27. David Page, *Prelude to Partition*, (Oxford, 1982), p. 76.
28. Ibid.
29. David Page, op. cit., p. 77.
30. *Bombay in 1921-22* : A review of the Administration of Presidency, pp. 2-3.

In September 1922, there was serious Hindu-Muslim riot at Multan in connection with the Muharram festival. In the year 1923, there occurred between 15 to 20 serious riots all over India, among which those of Amritsar, Lahore and Saharanpur figure prominently.[31] The first open outbreak was on the 11th July 1924 when an insignificant quarrel between some 'Kahar' Hindus and a Muhammadan boy occasioned a serious riot. This was followed in the next three days by a serious Mohammadan attack on Hindus. On the 15th, the Bakr-Id day a wild riot broke out again. The immediate cause of the trouble was that on the morning of the same day, local authorities proclaimed the closing of an additional route through the Hindu quarter for cows destined for slaughter. This order was resented by the Muslims, resulting in a serious riot. Sporadic attacks continued especially by the Muslim 'goondas' and temple was desecrated.[32]

The quite unprecedented growth of communal tension was in fact by far the most serious and permanent negative development of these years. There was a violent anti-Hindu outbrust in North-West Frontier Provinces. The recurrent ostensible issues were the Muslim demands for stopping 'music before mosque' and Hindu pressures for a ban on 'cow-slaughter.' Communal bodies proliferated and political alignments were made increasingly on a communal basis.[33]

Even at the height of Hindu-Muslim fraternization in 1919-22, Congress and Khilafat volunteer organisations had usually remained separate bodies, united because of the alliance between their leaders but politically divisive of the leaders' quarrel.[34] This unity at the uppear level was falsely based as it has been characterised as merely the marriage of convenience by some of the national leaders at that time. Very soon the hope of unity was defeated and again communal forces gained upper hand.

31. G.S. Ghurye, op. cit., p. 316.
32. G.S. Ghurye, op. cit , p. 316.
33. Sumit Sarkar, *Modern India 1885-1947*, (New Delhi, 1983), p. 233.
34. Ibid., pp. 233-35.

In 1928, riots at Bangalore, Surat, Nasik and Hyderabad were recorded. The major riots of Calcutta and Bombay, of 1926 and 1928 respectively resulted in very large number of casualties and damage to property. An aggravating cause in the Bombay riot was some labour disputes.[35] In Kishoreganj (Calcutta) subdivision, the young Comrades League had been active since 1929 in mobilising poor peasants against landlords and moneylanders, who were almost entirely Hindu.[36] It seems that an anti-Mahajan movement was about to develop. Under their auspices when, in April 1930, the post-Chittagong Armoury Raid removed all their leaders from the scene. Many Maulvies from Dacca and Noakhali immediately arrived to replace them and to continue the movement but under communal slogans. Their leadership was accepted by local villágers only after they had established their miracle making claims. Large scale and organised attacks on Mahajan houses spread rapidly and about 60 villages were affected. Snatching of debt bonds was the most prominent feature, accompanied quite often with plunder, loot, arson and sometimes even murder when Mahajans resisted strongly.[37]

A feature common to these riots is that they all occurred during an active phase of the national movement. This brings us to the question of the responsibility of the nationalist leaders and their failure to provide a broad political orientation to local Muslim grievances. Another strand in nationalist activities which reinforced a sense of insecurity among Muslims was the crop of physical-cultural associations or 'Akharas' for Hindu youths in Bihar and Bengal in mofussil towns; the presence of Hindu centres of 'lathi' and dagger play made Muslims nervous and stimulated similar preparations among them and it is clear from the establishment of Khaksar party in the Muslim community largely supported by the landlords.

35. *Indian Statutory Commission's Report* (1930), Vol. III, p. 68.
36. Tanika Sarkar's article, 'Communal Riots in Bengal,' in M. Hasan, (ed) *Communal and Pan-Islamic Trends in Colonial India*, (Delhi, 1981), p. 304.
37. Ibid., p. 305.

In the wake of spreading Hindu-Muslim bitterness 'Das pact' concluded in 1923 on the basis of substantial concessions to Muslims has rescinded in 1926 due to terrorist pressure.[38] The Das pact ensued amity at an elite level, but it could not check up communal organisations among up-country Hindus in Calcutta, particularly among the Marwaris which had the sanction of senior nationalist leaders like Malviya and Lala Lajpat Rai. The centre of communal propaganda was the predominantly Marwari trading areas in Calcutta. Since the Swarajists greatly depended on Marwari financial support, they tried to woo them with anti-korbani slogans. In Bihar also, in 1930 and even after that the involvement of Marwaris in proliferation and promotion of communal organisations can be marked.[39]

The reluctance of the orthodox Hindu politicians to make political profit out of the 'Suddhi' campaign led by the Arya Samajists was dictated by the nationalist political situation. When Gandhi suspended non-co-operation movement after Chauri-Chaura incident, Congress ranks became divided with regards to future policy.[40]

The preference for the policy of Das and Nehru involved a compromise over communal questions. Both Nehru and Das were basing their council entry programme on the same political alliance with the Khilafatists which Gandhiji had fostered during the non-co-operation movement and for Malviya and Chintamani to have their whole hearted support to the Arya Samaj, would have been to create communal divisions within the council entry party at a time when it needed to be strengthened. While Malviya and Chintamani flirted with the Arya Samaj in the period before 1923 elections, therefore they showed themselves more eager to come to terms with Nehru.[41]

38. M. Hasan, op. cit., p. 309.
39. L.S.S.O' Malley's, *Bihar and Orissa District Gazetteer, Patna* (Calutta, 1924), p. 59.
40. David Page, op. cit., pp. 76-77.
41. Ibid., p. 78.

To plot the connection between political ambitions at the provincial level and the growth of communal antagonisms in the localities is too ambitious a project to receive detailed attention here. It should be noted that while the coordination was poor, however local and provincial politcians did share common interests. The evidence for the connection between the political ambition and the stimulation of communal antagonisms is very evident even during the medieval period. But there are some people who negate any political connection with the communal problem.[42] In a speech delivered Hon'ble Srinivas Shastri, a political veteran remarks that,

> "There were riots even before any political ambitions began to emerge and the riots would remain in the country when all political ambitions were satisfied and the self-Government was fully established."[43]

The period of Civil Disobedience Movement witnessed repeated occurrences of communal riots. One may find an easy connection between the movement led by the Congress and fresh access of communal riots, but the conclusion would be highly misleading. One thing it must be pointed out that the 'riots were seen as an essential instrument by the imperial forces to check the political developments on the national plane.' Every nationalist step had to meet the spectre of communal violence and these negative developments were used to cow down the intense struggle for independence.[44] In 1931, again the communal violence reappeared on the national political scene. In 1931, in British administred India Benaras was disturbed in February. In 1932, Bombay again met the same fate. Two other places namely Alwar and Bundela in Hissar district figured as 'centres of communal ritos for the first time which took place in May had reverberations in the

42. *The Behar Herald*, dated September 25, 1926.
43. Ibid.
44. Sumit Sarkar, op. cit., p. 55.
For detail see Chapter VI in which it has been discussed how the imperialist forces used it as a weapon to check political advance on the national line.

next year on January 5.' The succeeding years also met with similar situation with regards to Hindu-Muslim relation.[45]

The immediate and the most ostensible issues of the violence that took place in different parts of the land, were '*music before mosque*' *and forcible* conversion of the lower class convert Muslims by the Hindus. The negative developments within Arya Samaj movement itself did not harass communal forces but itself was formulated and shaped by the most reactionary element who resisted any change.[46]

The new political setup, as the result of which the Indian National Congress came into power in 1937, produced a comparative bull in rioting activity. Only a few disturbances at the cattle fair in U.P. were reported. In 1939, however there was a recrudescence which began with a riot at Asansol, a railway junction in Bengal on 21st January. The next day Delhi witnessed a *clash and its repercussions* were felt in Kanpur on 11th February. The Kanpur affair started as an attack by Muslims on a Hindu marriage party and continued as a serious riot for some days. On 4th March 1939, in a number of towns in U.P. Hindus and Muslims clashed, the incident at Benaras being the most serious. On the occasion of holi, Benaras was again convulsed by a communal riot. On the 7th May, the riots at Calcutta accounted for 11 persons killed and over 90 injured. The Rathyatra festival brought in its wake a communal riot at Kanpur on 19th June. On the 4th October, Meerut registered a serious disturbance of peace. November witnessed a riot in an altogether quiet place in Sindh, Sukkur where the only communal disturbance of 1940 occurred on the 19th February. In 1941, Calcutta had the honour of beginning the trouble on the 8th February on the occasion of Muharram. The communal riot that started

45. G.S. Ghurye, *op. cit.* See the Chapter 'Communal Riots.'
46. Subsequent data have been collected from *Indian Annual Register* and *Indian Quarterly Register* annually published from Calcutta. The information listed above is cuelled from sources which cannot be expected to have reported all riots.

at Ahmedabad on 18th April did not subside for a long time. It was followed by a much more serious riot in Bombay city which started on 25th April and continued till 3rd June.

The four years beginning from 1942 were entirely quiet. However the year 1946 made up for all this. The expectancy of power transfer and a sort of frustrated feelings at its unsatisfactory nature are largely responsible for the large number of riots in that year. Ahmedabad, Calcutta, Allahabad, Bombay, Patna, Bhagalpur, Dacca are the main places where communal disturbances were felt in its ugly form. Those of Noakhali, Calcutta and Bombay were repeated more than once and were very serious

On the 15th August 1947 with the end of the British dominion in India, there emerged the two independent nations and countries of India and Pakistan. The behaviour of the two communities since that day for sometime thereafter is so abnormal owing to the very pecular and novel circumstances.

It is not possible within the scope of this study to investigate and explore the causes of communal disharmony on an all over India scale. Yet it is evident from a general survey, since the emergence of communalism in late nineteenth century Indian society, disputes among various trends within Hinduism or Islam did take place. The principal issues that came to the surface were cow protection and Urdu-Devanagari controversy.

'The demand for the use of the Devanagari script, first made by some Benaras Hindus in 1868 and granted by Lt. Governor Macdonnell in 1900 was connected with the tension between old and new elites of U.P.'[47] The cow protection movement also got its birth and popularity from Benaras. From here it passed on to the other provinces in Northern

47. Sumit Sarkar, op. cit., p. 79.

India.[48] The cow protection movement served as a link between elite and popular communalism, as Maclane has shown in his recent researches.[49]

The local Gorakshini Sabhas began springing up in many parts of northern India from the late 1880s, encouraged by the patronage of some lawyers and Zamindars, as well as the activities of some wandering mendicants.[50] These Sabhas became more militant and brought acute social tension.

On the other hand, Islamic revivalist trends were simultaneously insisting on the necessity of the Bakr-Id sacrifices. Muslim politicians feared that the Hindu majorities would further curb what was essential part of their religion. These two extreme views fostered reaction and counter-reaction at the social plane. And thus, the ground was prepared for the large scale riots of June-July 1893. Twenty-two serious communal disturbances did take place in Saran, Gaya and Patna districts in Bihar.[51] Riots were more organised in Ballia, where a Rajput Zamindar was extremely active.[52] In Bihar too, the initiatives were largely taken by the landed magnates. The cow was an age old religious symbol, but also the most vital economic asset for the peasant, apart from his land—which educated Hindus were attracted by the argument that cow protection would improve the health and prosperity of all Indians. The connection often assumed between revivalism and chauvinism appears a bit dubious in so far as the former led up to riots which Secretary of State Kimberley welcomed as 'cutting at the roots of the Congress agitation for the formation of united Indian people.'[53]

48. L S.S.O'Malley, *Bengal District Gozette*, *Muzaffarpur*, (Calcutta, 1907), p. 32.
49. Sumit Sarkar, op. cit., p. 80.
50. The organisation and function of the Gorakshini Sabhas have been discussed at length in Chapter III. How and why the Sabhas had been patronised by the vested interests has been shown in detail in Chapter V.
51. *Political Police Proceedings* (1890-95), pp. 6-23.
52. Gyan Pandey, "Rallying before the cow, the cause of Sectarian Strife in the Bhojpuri region 1886-1917" in *Social Scientist*, Oct. 1984, *Vol. XII, No. 10, pp. 18-20.*
53. See Sumit Sarkar, op. cit., p. 81.

3

History of Communal Riots-II

Communal Situation in Bihar (1890-1948)

It is a historical fact that Hindus and Muslims fought shoulder to shoulder against their common enemy i.e. British imperialism during the great uprising of 1857 even in the absence of modern political consciousness. Soon after the suppression of the revolt, the British officials had taken a particularly vindictive attitude towards the Muslim. In Delhi alone about 27,000 Muslims were hanged.[1] From now onwards, the Muslims were in general looked upon with suspicion. But this attitude soon changed in 1870's.[2] With the rise of nationalist movements, the British statesmen grew apprehensive about the safety and stability of their empire in India. To check the growth of a united national feeling in the country, they decided to follow more actively the policy of divide and rule,[3] and to divide the people along religious

1. Bipan Chandra, *Modern India*, (Delhi, 1977), p. 249.
2. Ibid.
3. *The Behar Herald*, July 30, 1927.
   Nearly four decades before the revolt of 1857 a British officer subscribing himself as "carnaticus" wrote in the "asiatic journal" for May 1821, 'Divide et impera' should be the motto of our Indian administration, whether political, civil or military.

lines, in other words to encourage communal and separatist tendencies in Indian politics.[4] The recurrent and spasmodic outbreak of communal riots in India was looked upon in England 'as a check to political advance.[5]

In this way, the imperialists hatched conspiracies in league with their Indian counterparts—Hindu and Muslim landlords, in defence of their respective vested interests. Since then, much emphasis was laid on the necessity of protecting cows and the 'Gorakshini Sabha' was founded all over India.[6] Consequently, the relations between Hindus and Muhammadans soon became strained in Bihar and other provinces, and in various parts the feeling aroused among the Hindus manifested itself in the rescue of cattle from Muhammadans in objecting to their slaughtering cattle and selling meat.[7] Not only this, but to give religious validity to the cow protection societies, certain stereotypes were being manufactured in the minds of the people by the vested interests. The people were made to believe that cows were sacred to Hindus and Hinduism found its sole expression in it. The ploughman's begging movement was launched which had its inception and spread among the villagers, may be attributed to the efforts of those interested in the Gorakshini agitation to keep the movement afloat.[8] Rumours were set in motion that Lord Mahadeo had imposed it to expiate the sin committed by the agricultural community in overworking their cattle.[9]

The cow protectors were active in inciting communal riots. There are numerous instances of communal riots well planned and organised by these elements of the society. In

4. *The Behar Herald*, Sept. 25, 1926.
   A speech delivered by the Right Hon'ble Srinivas Shastri on 'Communal problem in India.'
5. Ibid.
6. V.C.P., Choudhary, *Secularism Versus Communalism*, (Patna, 1977) p. 22.
7. L.S.S.O'Malley's, *Bengal District Gazetteers : Muzaffarpur* (Calcutta, 1907), pp. 32-33.
8. Ibid.
9. Ibid-

fact a short intimation from the cow protectors could mobilise people from 2000 to 7000. Many a time the rioters came on horses, cycle and elephants from different areas to do the actual fighting. An organised riot on the false propaganda that a cow is to be sacrificed, was apprehended on 24th April 1929 at Katwar village (Saran). Within an hour the people assembled calling 'Gao Mata ki Jay' from the neighbouring villages: Patar, Sasaram, Mahmadpur and Katwar. They assembled there at the instigation of Babu Rajendra Prasad of Lohganj, an influential person of the locality and happened to be an active person in the cow protection movement.[10] But the incident could fortunately be localised and no any happeing of untoward nature did take place as the rioters came to know that no any sacrifice did take place.[11]

In most of the cases, the initiatives regarding cow protection were taken by Hindu vested interest groups but the examples of the Muslims using it as a pretext do not lack. The riot of this nature (at the instigation of a Muslim) did take place at the village Ramde Chapra (Arrah). In this village there was an old clash between the two parties of Mahammadans. One of them incited the Hindus to object to the beef being brought for a marriage feast.[12]

The butchers driving their cattle along the road became an object of suspicion and was challenged accordingly. In March 1895, a serious riot broke out in the village of Mathurapur in the Sheohar thana. The Hindus attacked Muslims on the plea that the Muhammadans of the village intended to sacrifice a calf at the mosque on the occasion of the Id-ul-Fitr.'[13] Such an interference with village customs caused considerable feeling of tension throughout the whole

10. *Political Special File No.* 52/1929 (B.S.A.).
11. Ibid.
12. *Political Special File No.* 115/1928 (B S.A.).
    See extract from the Confidential Diary of S.P. Shahabad dated 2.5. 1928.
13. L.S S.O'Malley's, *Bengal District Gazetteers : Muzaffarpur*, Calcutta (1907), p. 32.

province. The Gorakshini Sabha and elaborate nature of the penance under ploughmen's begging movement give reason to believe that it had been 'carefully thought out.'[14]

Primarily, the landlords had their main concern with the Gorakshini Sabha but during the period 1924-25, it had been chiefly supported by Marwaris and other members of the merchant class who displayed more favour than most of their correligionists towards the object of Hindu veneration.[15] There were some Muslim organisations too, such as 'Anjuman Islamia' which dealt mainly with social and religious questions.[16]

Since the formation of Gorakshini Sabha and the introduction of ploughman's begging movement, it would not be an exaggeration to say that the incidents of communal rioting have become a regular feature of life. At several times, the members of the Gorakshini sabha instigated and perpetuated crimes. On 17th April 1890, a riot of serious nature did take place on the occasion of fair in the Barahpur village under the instigation of Gopalnand Swami, a member of the Benaras Gorakshini Sabha.[17] At Nurnagar (Chaptra) the existing peace was disrupted on 30th March 1891. In this case, Muslims were attacked by a large Hindu mob resulting in loot and arson.[18]

Once the social fabric of communal harmony was disrupted, it generated tension in the society. Hinduism found its expression in the protection of cows and 'music before the mosque' did not appeal to the Muslims because to them it was anti-Islamic. Processions were being organised by one community to antagonise the members of other community. Processions organised and led by Hindus alienated the Muslim

14. Ibid.
15. L S.S.O'Malley's, *Bihar and Orissa District Gazetteers : Patna*, (Calcutta, 1924), p. 59.
16. Ibid.
17. *Political Police Proceeding* (1891-95)(B.S A.) p. 6.
18. Ibid.

community and on the other hand any act by the Muslim community appeared challenge to Hinduism. It was a quite recent development, otherwise previously Muslims and Hindus shared one another's customs and religious ceremonies.[19]

On 10th July 1891, in Phulwarisharif (Patna) the riot originated in consequence of the Muhammadans attempting to stop the 'Rathyatra' procession.[20] In 1892, starting from the month of July to November, Patna, Chapra and Saran districts remained the centres of trouble. In most of the cases, the trouble centred round cow-killing and music before mosque.[21]

In the succeeding years communal virus spread in different other districts of the province consequent to the circulation of the literature on the issue of protecting cows. In 1893, Nawada, Gaya and Aurangabad became centres of communal antagonisms.[22] In most cases, the riots were instigated or financed by the landlords and some other influential persons of the areas.

On 25th March, 1893 a trouble did take place at Katia Taur (Aurangabad). The trouble originated when some Hindus did waylaid a Muhammadan who was taking home a bullock. The Muhammadans appealed that they were not taking away the bullock with the intention of sacrifice but were not heard...the Hindus snatched and took away the animal headed by a dependent of the Maharaja of Deo.[23]

19. L.S.S.O'Malley's, *Bihar and Orissa District Gazetteers : Patna*, (Calcutta, 1924), p. 63.
Hindus and Muslims did adopt some religious customs of their rival community. Muslims also observed the Hindu practice of launching 'Paper boats' on the Ganges after marriage or birth. In Patna, among the "Panch Pir" two are Hindu names.
20. *Political Police Proceeding* (1891-95), p. 4.
21. Ibid.
22. Ibid.
23. *Political Police Proceeding* (1891-95), p. 4 (B.S.A.). Also see V.C.P. Choudhary, op. cit., p. 23.

In this case the involvement of the landlord is quite evident. It must not be forgotten that the masses of the two communities desired to live amicably. But more often, the peaceful relation between the masses of the two communities was disturbed by the vested interests after arousal of vicious propaganda and rumours.

Muslim landlords similarly participated in communal riots. At Hilsa on 26th June 1893, the Muslim subdivisional officer of Bihar who was present there at the time, sought assistance from the neighbouring Muhammadan landlords . . . and have committed violence on Hindus . . . with a 'large body' of the retainers of Muslim landlords.[24] It is interesting to note that most of the pepole responsible for these crimes went 'scotfree' as the bureaucracy and judiciary in league with landlords and imperialists abetted and perpetuated such crimes.

In the same year, riots did occur at several other places—at Masaurhi in Patna, Bhusunda in Gaya, Tikari, Sherghati and Nawada. It is also to be noted that the cattle fairs became the source of conflict.[25] It is during these days the rising prices and its effects were being felt in daily lives of the people. The mounting prices did largely affect the prices of cattle also which were previously available at cheaper rates. The Hindu traders as well as the agriculturist were made to believe that the reason behind the rising prices of cattle was the slaughter of animals by the Muslims on a large scale.

The real cause behind the Hindu-Muslim riot was not

24. Ibid.
25. Barahpur, Sonepur, Ainkhaon, were the main cattle fairs in North and South Bihar. Tension persisted at these centres in selling and purchasing of cattle which soon assumed communal shape.
In Dec. 11, 1915, it was reported that "The Sonepur fair was a tame affair for this year also but the action of H.H. Maharaja of Rewan in stopping cow slaughter is commendable . . ."—*The Behar Herald*, Dec. 11, 1915.

the issue of cow slaughter. Neither cows were very sacred to Hindus before the spread of Gorakshini Sabha. If Hindus were bent upon saving the lives of cows and checking the Muslims daring so due to any religious affiliations, why not they were so instrumental in their actions when cows were being slaughtered on a large scale on behalf of the Englishmen for whom the beef was a favourite dish? Mahatma Gandhi in the course of his long speech delivered on the issue of Hindu-Muslim tension in India spoke,

> "I have never been able to understand the antipathy towards the musalmans on that score. We say nothing about the slaughter that daily takes place on behalf of Englishmen. Our anger becomes hot when a musalman slaughters a cow."[26]

The moot question behind the trouble was not cow sacrifice due to any religious affiliations of Hindus with cow. But the lower middle class Hindus who were facing rising prices in their daily lives and cattle being a great asset of agrarian economy were much affected. On the other hand, lower middle class section of the Muslim community who engaged themselves in trade were in favour of cow slaughter as leather was one of the commodities exclusively for them. The upper class Muslims were laying emphasis, side by side with the Hindus on the protection of cattle.[27] It was because their interests were seldom threatened due to these movements, so they did happily join the movements for protection of cattle.

There was a complete lull for about ten years and almost no any communal riot of serious nature was reported. During these periods, it seemed that communal tension had gone into

26. *The Behar Herald*, 7th June 1924.
    The text of Gandhiji's speech published under the heading 'Hindu-Muslim Entente.'
27. *The Behar Herald*, Dec. 11, 1915.
    Letter to the editor by some Muslims—"we are assured that the educated and high class Muhammadans are always in favour of it . . . . It is the only low caste Muslims who take liberty."

hibernation but the partition of Bengal in 1905 was followed by a recurrent and also more violent form of communal riots. One of the objectives of the partition was to divide Hindu and Muslim Bengali to weaken the tide of national movement. The year after the partition was followed by the establishment of All India Muslim League in 1906.

The communal disturbances were not a regular feature of life in India in the 19th century. But in the 20th century the picture has gradually changed. The Government of India in their memorandum to the Indian statutory commission, mentions riots at several places on the all India scale.[28] The frequency of riots increased during the 1920s and every province was affected, Bihar and Bengal being the worse victims.[29] The answer to this question should be sought in the political developments of this period. During the period, more often the communal riots were planned, organised and well financed by socio-religious organisations, landlords and bureaucrats. These vested interest groups were nurtured by the imperialists whose sole purpose was to check the tide of national movement. On the other hand, landlords often used it as a potent weapon to bring disunion among the exploited peasants and the big factory owners with their class interests threatened, conformed to the principle of using this parochial and obscurantist social and religious movements to cause disunion among the exploited workers.

A communal riot of this nature has been reported from the Sagi village in Begusarai on 21st Nov. 1912. The immediate cause of the trouble was 'Kurbani.' But the incident was a peculiar one, in the sense that the result of this incident was not confined to itself but had a tendency to transend its own limited areas. The strangest part of this episode was that 'a certain' Mr. Macdonald, an owner of a

28. *Report of the Indian Statutory Commission*, Vol. IV, Part I (Calcutta, 1930), pp. 97-107.

29. The major riots of 1920s are considered in G.R. Thursby, *Hindu-Muslim Relation in British Iudia*, Leiden, 1975).

Daulatpur factory close to Sagi . . . who is said to have great influence in the locality, hired some goonda elements and instigated them to do the actual disturbance.[30]

Another significant development of this period was that our leaders were quite disillusioned and all their hopes of political concessions were belied. The introduction of Morley-Minto reforms further intensified the situation. Mr. Mazherul Haq, one of the Muslim League members discussed in a meeting,

> "The Morley-Minto reforms may or may not have satisfied the aspirations of educated Indians . . . . it whipped their political lethargy and gave them ample opportunities to display their activities in the sphere of politics."[31] Mr. Haq further goes on saying that 'when the controversy generated by Morley-Minto reforms was about to an end, the announcement of 'separate electorate' did much more damage to the cause of Hindu-Muslim relation.'

Due to these political developments, anti-British feeling was gathering momentum during this period. In October 1917 riot did take place in Shahabad on the occasion of Bakr-Id.[32] Shahabad had been the scene of massive outbreak of rioting described by observers as 'unprecedented since 1857-58'. It seems to have been made at the instance of the two co-owners of the village who happened to be present at the meeting of pleaders, merchants and other 'influential gentry' that decided on organising such a demonstration apparently as part of an effort to build up nationalist and public activities in the district.[33] The proprietors of

30. *The Behar Herald*, Dec. 5, 1912.
Published private letter written by Charles R. Macdonald to Mr. Hoernle, subdivisional Magistrate, Begusarai.
31. *The Behar Herald*, Jan. 15, 1916.
32. *The Behar Herald*, Oct. 13, 1917.
33. *Political Special File No.* 112/1918 (R.S.A.) See Published Oldham Report on the Bakr-Id disturbance. Also see, Gyanendra Pandey's. 'Sectarian and other Solidarities : Some observations on communal mobilisation in Modern India,' in *Proceedings of the 40th Session of Indian History Congress*, (Waltair, 1979), pp. 625-627.

Ibrahimpur probably recommended it as the venue for demonstration because of a long standing grudge against the Muslims of the village, though the village had been transferred to them many generations ago, the tenants had remained loyal to the original Muslim maliks.[34]

However the 'limited' demonstration assumed unexpectedly large proportions and led after the performance of Kurbani under official protection at Ibrahimpur and neighbouring villages of Milki and Bhagalpur. Officials spoke of veritable war and acknowledged that over a hundred and fifty square miles had passed into the hands of the rebels.[35]

Some of the circumstances surrounding the outbreak are significant. Several witnesses stated before the Tribunal Courts held afterwards at Arrah and Gaya that they were under the belief that the British Raj was ending. A number of accused complained that they had gone to the scene of fighting in order to see the armies of the Raja of Rewan and there were reports that 'Bengalis' were also coming to help. The evidence shows that the rioting crowds were shouting 'Angrez ka Raj uth gaya' and 'German ki jay.'[36]

This circulation of nationalist rumours was only one of the surprising aspects of the communal uprising of 1917. Local officials noted that the part of Shahabad that burst into flame in 1917 'almost exactly coincided with the area affected in 1857-58,'[37] and the indications are that many of the same links and loyalties were operative in the process of mobilisation. It may be merely a coincidence, one official observed that 'The Jagdishpur family with its branch at Dallipur, the

34. L S.S.O'Malley's, *Shahabad District Gazetteer*, (Calcutta, 19 4), p. 143.
35. *Political Special File No.* 112/1918 (B.S.A.). See, Confidential Letter No. 168/1-C to Macpherson, Chief Secretary, Govt. of Bihar.
36. Ibid. See, Oldham's Report (Commissioner, Patna Division) dated 31 Dec. 1917, pp. 17-18.
37. Ibid.

descendants and relatives of the family of Kunwar Singh who was acknowledged to be associated in popular rumour with the disturbances in 1917'. Several persons actually heard the mob calling out 'Dallipur Ke Babu Ki Jai.'[38] The prominence of the upper caste people involved in the trouble was also marked upon. They , consisted mainly of Rajputs, and Bhumihars.[39] The Hindus concerned in these disturbances are a very strong community, an official reported on 29 September 1917, the day after the first outbreak of rioting.[40] Thus the Bakr-Id riots of Shahabad and Gaya show more than anything else the extreme we have come for want of popular responsibility and popular Government.[41]

The relations between Hindus and Muslims in Bihar were severely strained on numerous occasions in the succeeding years, despite the efforts of political leaders to encourge mutual forbearance and unity. From this period on a new cause, namely religious conversions, came to be added to the existing sources of conflict. New militant organisations of Hindus; Suddhi and Sangathan launched by the Arya Samaj, and Tanjeem and Tabligh among the Muslims added to the scale of communal violence.[42]

It is not our sole purpose to stigmatise Arya Samaj. If any comment is necessary, it is that the 'Sudhi' movement was not unprovoced. In all probability, it was a Hindu reaction to the superior powers of mobilisation demonstrated by the Muslims during the Khilafat movement. What is equally important, however, is that it appears to

38. *Bihar and Orissa Police Abstract of Intelligence 1917*, p. 334. Also see, Oldham's Report, pp. 20-21.

39. See *Oldham Report* (File No. 112/1918), Appendix IX.

40 P. Robb, ' Officials and non-officials as leaders in popular agitation: Shahabad 1917 and conspiracies." in B.N. Pandey (ed), *Leadership in South Asia*, (Delhi, 1977), p. 182.

41. *The Behar Herald*, Nov. 10, 1917.
Text of Rai Bahadur P.N. Sinha's speech on Shahabad and Gaya disturbances.

42. G.R. Thursby, op. cit., p. 120.

have been religious in origin. Swami Shradhanand one of its main instigators, had certainly played prominent role in the scenes of fraternization in Delhi in 1919. But though many Hindu politicians had become disenchanted with Gandhi's policy of Hindu-Muslim unity after the Malwar disturbances of 1921, there is little evidence to suggest that any of them lent whole-hearted support to Shradhanand in 1923.[43]

The relations between Hindus and Muslims in Bihar were severely strained during the year 1923 and at several places untoward incidents did occur.[44] The main source of dissension was the conversion of musalman Rajputs to the Arya Samaj creed in the province, and fears were entertained by the more orthodox Muhammadans that the movement would spread to Shahabad.[45]

To combat this attack on their faith, funds were collected and Muhammadan preachers despatched to oppose the Hindu missionaries action, which in turn provoked counter propaganda from Hindus and mutual recriminations were felt not only in Shahabad but in the neighbouring districts of Saran, Muzaffarpur, Monghyr and Patna.[46] The year has seen no improvement in the general relations between the people of the two communities, beyond an attempted rapproachment between the less orthodox believers on both sides.[47] The causes are not so far to seek. To some extent this problem was connected with Congress politics.[48] A good deal of resentment was felt in Muhammadan circles at what was regarded as an attempt to convert the Congress into a Hindu organisation.[49]

43. David Page, *Prelude to Partition*, (Oxford, 1982), p. 76.
44. *Administrative Report to the Govt of Bihar and Orissa*, (1923-24), p. 6.
45. Ibid.
46. Ibid.
47. Ibid., p. 7.
48. Ibid.
49. *Administrative Report to the Govt of Bihar and Orissa* (1924-25), p. 4.

During these periods, the feelings run very high in the Muslim community regarding the character of the Congress party. The confusion became worse confounded and the tension was increased by recriminations which passed between the two communities regarding the alleged misapplication of Congress funds.[50] On the other hand Muhammadans were keenly disappointed at the result of the district board elections, in which hardly any of their candidates were successful. In view of the exacerbation of feeling which continued previously in many parts of the province, and the repeated occurrences of petty incidents on the occasions of Bakr-Id and Ram Naomi festivals, calculated to provoke the outbreak of violent disturbances in Patna, Bhagalpur, Shahabad and also at several other plaees.[51] It must be commented here that the tension ensued out of the 'political ambition' of the middle class Hindu and Muslim members who otherwise lost their seats in district board election and their hold in Congress, shifted to the short term solutions of the problem.

To plot the connection between political ambitions at the provincial level and the growth of communal antagonisms in the localities is too ambitious a project to receive detailed attention here. It should be noted that while the coordination was poor, however local and provincial politicians did share common interests. The evidence for the connection between the political ambition and the stimulation of communal antagonism is very evident from the perusal of available records. But the extent to which the politicians were responsible for provoking the riot is uncertain.

After discussing the role of politically ambitious individuals in short, it seems here all the more necessary to point out the changing base of communal riots. Previously, most of the communal riots had rural base but from these periods onwards it gradually assumed urban centres. The question

50. Ibid.
51. Ibid.

of cow slaughter was giving way to the problem of music before mosque. In rural areas, communal riots were chiefly organised and financed by the landlords in their vested class interests for diverting the resentment of the rural masses against Zamindari oppression, taxation and moneylending. Now the same role has been played by the politically ambitious groups to make their political fortunes out of communal tension. The sentiments of the masses were being aroused by these elements through vicious propaganda.

Up to 1926-27, several provinces in the country were haunted by the black cloud of communal bitterness. In Bihar too, as elsewhere, the strife continued to darken the political horizon. A strong impetus was given to the forces which make for discord by the serious Calcutta riots at the very beginning of this period.[52] Some of the combatants returning from Calcutta to their homes in Bihar with mark of injury were greeted as heroes.[53] Hindus and Muslims alike were laying in secret stores of lathis and other weapons, not so much with the definite idea of taking the offensive, but out of 'fear psychosis' with regard to the intentions of the other sides.[54]

In fact, the most marked result of the Calcutta riots was to accentuate to an almost fantastic degree the prevailing atmosphere of nervousness in both communities. Any rumour of aggression by the opposite party, however absurd, obtained ready credence, and the chief danger was that some panic, arising out of a rumour wholly without foundation, would develop into a serious trouble.[55] The tension existed in the whole province apart from any religious questions. At several places riots occurred out of petty quarrels between the individuals of the two communities. In the existing state of

52. *Administrative Report to the Govt. of Bihar & Orissa* (1926-27), pp. 5-7.
53. Ibid.
54. Ibid.
55. Ibid.

nervousness, the anti-social elements seized on the opportunity and during the 48 hours there was much fighting, bloodshed and anarchy.[56] Several places were declared disturbed and special police force was quartered. The vexed questions of music before mosque and the deliberate defilement of mosques and temples were given currency at the mass level. Patna, Gaya, Saran, Monghyr, Darbhanga, Sasaram and Santal Pargana were the worst sufferers.[57]

In this state of anarchy and the breakdown of law and order, the murder of Swami Shradhanand provided fuel to the fire. The Hindus in most of the large towns observed 'hartals' in his memory, and there was a good deal of rather excited oratory which brought the situation more tense.[58] This resulted in the boycott of the festivals of one community by the other which previously had been shared and enjoyed together. For example, in several districts the Hindus entirely abstained from participating the Muharram festival.[59] It was also not unprovoked. The leaders of the Hindu Mahasabha were more instrumental during these days. At several places. the peaceful and harmonious daily lives of the people was largely disrupted by the activities of the Arya Samajists who with their divine 'suddhi' campaign insisted more and more on conversion and compensation of low caste people to the Hindu creed. The communal riot in Bettiah which took place on 4th August 1927 was consequent to the activities of the Arya Samajists.[60] The Bettiah disturbances undoubtedly embittered feelings in the Tirhut division. The peculiar feature of the Bettiah riot lies in the fact that a new kind of provocation ensued i.e. resemblance of Muharrum procession to Mahabiridal procession. This type of provocation was quite absent in the previous years.[61]

56. Ibid.
57. Ibid.
58. Ibid.
59. *Administrative Report to the Govt. of Bihar & Orissa* (1927-28), Chapter I, p. 1.
60. *Political Special File No.* 216/1927, p. 9 (B.S.A.).
61. Ibid.

The year 1928-29 saw no any improvement in the general condition of the people. Antagonism between the Hindus and the Muhammadans was again a prominent feature of the political lanscape. On the occasion of Bakr-Id, the breach of peace resulting in serious fracas did take place at several places; Gaya, Patna, Muzaffarpur and Bhagalpur being the worst sufferers. Large scale looting and arson did take place. It has been mentioned in the Government records that the number of murders licensed in 1928 was considerably more than double that recorded in the previous year.[62] At several places where the riots occurred the local rural police force did nothing in checking the trouble and became the silent spectators of the whole tragic dramas. The police was conniving with the rioters at several places.[63]

It is to be noted here that the period was followed by the massive rise in prices, acute unemployment and extremely poor and worsening condition of the people consequent to the world-wide economic depression. The poor peasants were fighting against oppression and the lower middle class in particular were in a position to believe that they would face the problem of being declassed. The constant fear of the loss of their socio-economic position provided acute social tension which saw its manifestation in communal riots. It happened not incidentally but the different political as well as communal organisations could be held responsible. The masses at large were made to believe that their present economic condition .was due to the participation of the members of the rival community in profession, trade and menial labours. (It has been discussed at length in Chapter IV).

Another point which needs some discussion here is the urban base of communal riots. Up to these periods, the

62. *Administrative Report to the Govt. of Bihar & Orissa* (1928-29), p. 2.
63. *Political Special File No.* 115/1928. Special Report of Crime, Schedule XLVII, Form no. 23.

communal question became basically the petty-bourgeoisie problem. At the mass level in the rural areas there was still some element of communal harmony. At several occasions in the villages, the Hindus participated in the Muharram festival but kept aloof in the towns.[64]

Looking ahead to the coming constitutional changes, a number of provincial Muhammadan leaders were engaged in organising opposition to the Nehru Report. A new provincial Muslim conference was formed and on the press and platform the Nehru report was denounced as detrimental to the Muslim interests.[65]

In the succeeding years, the general situation showed general improvement due to the efforts of the Government. The Muhammadans particularly became aggressive after the massacres that followed in March 1931. Now onwards, there was a good deal of talk of the setting up of a parallel institution.[66] The Mohammadans in general were adopting the policy of keeping themselves aloof from the agitations that was being led by the nationalist Congressmen. At several places, the riots originated out of this fact. A riot occurred in Champaran district in September 1931 because the local Muhammadans refused to join the agitation.[67] There was friction over the Ram Navmi procession in Hazaribagh, and at the Bakr-Id there was a riot in Shahabad where since 1917 the feeling always runs very high.[68]

Any action by the Muslim regarding national movement largely apprehended the colonial rulers. In this way, the loyalist elements had now to be encouraged to take to politics, but only to constitutional and parliamentary and dependent politics. Accordingly, the ready acceptance by the British

64. *Administrative Report to the Govt. of Bihar & Orissa* (1929-30), pp. 4-5.
65. Ibid.
66. *Administrative Report to the Govt. of Bihar & Orissa* (1930-31), p. 11.
67. Ibid,
68. Ibid.

authorities in 1906 of Muslim communal demands and of the claim of the upper communal leaders of being representatives of all Muslims had, in part, the objective of preventing Muslims from taking to political agitation and joining the Congress.[69] It is wrong to describe this policy of the Government as 'Pro-Muslim.' Rather, its aim was to keep upper and middle class Muslims pro-British.

The movement led by Congress along national lines was described by the rulers as detrimental to the cause of Muslim demands. In this way, the Civil Disobedience Movement launched by Mahatma Gandhi and other nationalist leaders was taken to be 'one of the harmful acts which had widened the gulf between the two communities.'[70] Consequently, the Muhammadans as a community never approved of the movement, on the other hand the Congress persisted it in spite of Muhammadan's disapproval sometimes leading to the breach of peace between the two communities.[71] The tension persisted in Patna, Bhagalpur, Monghyr and Muzaffarpur but did not assume wide proportions.

The policy of supporting parliamentary and dependent communal politics was followed from 1906. Whenever communalism tended to become militant or to come closer to the nationalist forces, it was cold-shouldered or even opposed. Jinah was never the official favourite and was treated virtually at par with the Congress leaders from 1930 to 1934. Nor was communalism given all out support till 1939, even though it was made major issue and sedulously natured through sympathy, consideration and concessions during the constitutional discussions of 1930-34. It was also already seen as the most important political weapon against the burgeoning national movement.

After 1937, the British shifted from balanced to

69. Bipan Chandra, op. cit., p. 256.
70. *Administrative Report to the Govt. of Bihar & Orissa* (1932-34), p. 13.
71. Ibid., p. 14.

uncontrolled communalism, encouraged total communal division, gave virtually open support to the Muslim League especially in its anti-Congress role and tolerated its efforts to acquire a mass character. From now onwards, communalism and communal riots were a mix. The coming of Jinnah in Bihar caused considerable communal tension in the province. A communal riot that did take place on 7th May 1939 in Gaya was consequent to the Jinnah's arrival. The history of the communal troubles in Gaya dated back to the year 1937, when a communal riot took place in Aurangabad.[72] The tension was laeer accentuated by the demonstrations made in the same year on the arrival of Mr. Jinnah at Gaya, where an armed procession was taken out. Since then the local leaders of the Muslim League were engaged in an intensive campaign which had tended to promote communal hatred against the rival community.[73] Towards the end of the year 1938, the speeches delivered in the session of the Provincial Muslim League in which the two communities were painted as two separate entities having no affinity with each other and in which the responsibility for the alleged injustices and inequality of the Musalmans were flung upon the shoulders of the Government, fanned and fed the communal bitterness.[74] The preaching of the Muslims that religion was in danger since the assumption of office by the Congress and that the Congress Government was synonymous with Hindu Government greatly excited the Muslim population.

Congress leaders proclaimed the non-communal character of thir organisation in order to enlist the support of various castes and communities living in India. The policy was vital in a divided and disperate country like India. Indeed the claim of being a national body could only be sustained by

72. Valmiki Choudhary (ed , *Dr. Rajendra Prasad Correspondence and Select Documents*, (New Delhi, 1984), Vol. 3, p. 334. 'Statements of facts made in the Assembly on behalf of the Govt. by Mr. K.B. Sahay, Parliamentary Secretary in the Bihar Legislative Assembly on 16th May 1939.'
73. Ibid., p. 335.
74. Ibid.

transcending, at least in theory, caste and sectarian boundaries.[75] Besides by adopting the non-communal posture Congress hoped to allay the apprehension of certain groups: particularly the Muslims, about the Hindu Character of the organisation. Thus the attempt to pass a resolution at the 1887 Congress calling for cow-killing to be made a penal offence was thwarted; instead it was decided to avoid discussion on any subject to which either Hindu or Muslim delegates 'unanimously' or nearly unanimously were opposed.[76] The consternation caused by this attempt led Surendra Nath Benerjee to assure Muslims that the Congress movement was of 'United India', of Hindus and Muhammadans, of Parsis and Sikhs. . . . Here we have all agreed to bury our differences.[77] Such assurances were not matched by practice. The Congress, in spite of its secular protestations, was quite often drawn into activities or associations pioneered by Hindu revivalists.

This factor became more evident at the Provincial level where all political parties and organisations largely dwelt on the election prospect. Though, the Congress leaders at several occasions condemned the ideologies and programmes of the Hindu Mahasabha with a view not to lose Muslim support in the provinces. At several times, the Hindu Sabha and its active supporters had been held responsible for communal tension. Up to 1945, the political scenario of the country forced even the secular organisations to join forces with the 'Communal and reactionary' organisations. The Congress leaders proclaimed 'electoral alliance' with the Hindu Mahasabha to safeguard their electoral fortune. The pact on this line was initiated by Rajendra Prasad, one of the active Congress workers. But the idea was resented by Jawaharlal

75. For instance, Ajudhia Nath Kunzru, a leading pleader in Allahabad during 1880s said, "Congress works not for the good of this class or that class, nor of this or that province but for the benefit of the whole nation." *Tribune* (Lahore), dated 23rd June 1889.
76. See an article by M. Hasan, in Communal and . . . , p. 197.
77. Ibid.

Nehru not to maintain secular character of the Congress but out of fear of losing Muhammadan support in the Muhammadan majority provinces. In a letter to Mr. Rajendra Prasad, Jawaharlal Nehru clearly pointed out,

> "Just at present the Congress prestige is very great and so far as general seats are concerned there is hardly any doubt that we shall capture the lot. There is practically no chance of a Hindu Sabha candidate winning against a Congress candidate. Our main contest is going to be for the Muslim seats. . . . Any formal or informal arrangements with the Hindu Sabha will have far-reaching repercussions on the Muslim electorate. The Muslim League will exploit this situation fully and again emphasize, as they have done in the past, that the Congress is Hindu Mahasabha in different guise.[78]

These political developments had very harmful effect on the existing peace at the mass level. It plunged the whole province into general trend of thinking of 'Hindu votes' and 'Muslim votes.' On the other hand, the planning of 'Partition' filled the sense of acute anger among the Hindu population. The communal forces were let loose and at places they got support from the local officials. At several places, the local Government officials were conniving with the anti-social elements who often did bring misery to the people. A prominent Congress worker deputed by Mr. Rajendra Prasad was reported to have told a gathering of Hindus at the Fatwah High School., Patna on September 27, 1946, 'I am one of the 86 persons deputed by Dr. Rajendra Prasad . . . and this is the right time for us to destroy and annihiliate our enemies.'[79]

78 A letter from Jawahar Lal Nehru to Rajendra Prasad against electoral alliance with the Hindu Mahasabha, 6 Oct. 1945 in B.N. Pandey (ed), *The Indian Nationalist Movement . Select Documents* (Delhi, 1979), p. 172.

79. Extract from the Verbatim Copy of *The Morning News* Report dated 20th October 1946 regarding Fatwah meeting. Also see, *The Bihar State Killing* (1946). Published official statement and Resolution of Bihar Provincial Muslim League on Bihar massacre, pp. 4-9.

In this way, an atmosphere of confidence ensued among the goonda elements and they were free to do anything. Many criminals known to authority and the police alike openly instigated the crimes or actually took part in them. They were moving freely being confident that they will not be brought to book.[80]

The anti-Muslim arrogant and callous attitude of many Hindu officials who were dealing with the cases arising out of the great massacre of the November riots, was quite evident. In many cases it so happened that though the majority of the Muslims were killed, survivors have been arrested on charges of arson, murder, loot etc. while those Hindu goondas who actually did the killing were scot-free or arrested and let off on bail.[81]

A typical example of how the officials were behaving is given below:[82]

Some Muslim residents of village Rupahua in Monghyr district appeared as prosecution witness . . . when these Muslims were narrating how even children have been massacred, the high police officer immediately interrupted and said that this was 'revenge for Noakhali.' One of the officers used abusive language.

During the period of this infighting going on between the Hindus and the Muslims, 'in many places they seized lawfully held arms of the Muslims on the assurance that they were to protect them, and then quietly withdrew from the scene of occurrence and allow the Muslims to be butchered.' On the other hand, Hindus were allowed to retain their licences secretly. Not only this, when all the Hindus as well as Muslim shops were closed by the Government, one of the relatives of the Premier, Bihar approached the District Magistrate for licence. The DM ordered his licence clerk to issue a licence

80 *The Bihar State Killing* (1946), p. 5.
81. *The Dawn*, February 1, 1946.
82. Ibid.

which was handed over to the Premier's nephew without any enquiry into the character of the applicant which is the general rule.[83]

Besides, rumour mongers did play very significant role in igniting communal fury in the province. At several places meetings were being held in public under the shadow of the Government officials, where the refugees from Punjab could present their exaggerated view of Punjab happening. It is said that Mr. Sudan, the Assessment Officer of the Notified Area Committee, Mokameh addressed a meeting and discussed the massacre of Punjabi Hindus which had very bad impression on people's mind.[84]

All these actions of the Government officials went unnoticed because the 'imperial ruler seated at the centre enjoyed the fun of the Congress ministry getting discredited.' They had to convince the people that the claim of their leaders to rule the country by their own people and in their own interests was farce. To follow this maxim, all anti-social elements and the communal forces were let loose. Belied and frustrated Nehru wrote a letter to Vallabh Bhai Patel in which he maintained that,

> "... In the affected areas (Patna, Gaya and Monghyr districts), there has been a definite attempt on the part of Hindu mobs to exterminate the Muslims. He further says, the local officials in many places and especially the I.C.S. elements brought much damage."[85]

On the other hand, Jinnah's call for 'Direct Action' disrupted the very fabric of social harmony. 'As a result of Jinnah's call for Direct Action which was publicly celebrated

83. Extract from *The Dawn* dated 5.5.47. 'Techniques of Riots in Bihar : Planned Attacks : Police Support.'
84. *Political Special File No.* 23(1)/1747, Part II (B.S.A.).
85. Letter from Jawahar Lal Nehru to Vallabh Bhai Patel on the Bihar riots dated 5th Nov. 1946, in B.N. Pandey (ed), op. cit. p. 203.

by the Muslim League Government of Bengal on 16th August 1946, the riot spread to Hindu majority provinces of Bihar where the Hindus retaliated against the Muslims.'[86]

86. Ibid.

4

Communal Riots vis-a-vis Class Struggle

It has been discussed in the previous chapter that communal identity and division has always pervaded Indian society but communalism is one of the byproducts of colonial underdevelopment of Indian economy.[1] The rise of modern politics and social classes occurred in the same period and the crisis of colonial economy began to be largely felt. Colonial economy, underdevelopment and economic stagnation produced conditions 'conducive to the growth of internal division and antagonism within society.'[2] These internal divisions promoted violence and social tension at the mass level. It is to be noted that why the lower class frustration often led to violence in contrast to the middle and upper class sections. For the masses, communal violence was sometimes a 'substitute' for class struggle due to the lack of class consciousnes at the mass level. Moreover a large number of the urban poor, victims and products of colonial underdevelopment, were declassed, rootless, lumpen whose social anger and acute sense

1. Bipan Chandra, *Communalism in Modern India*, (New Delhi, 1984), p. 1.
2. Ibid., p. 34.

of deprivation invariably found expression in senseless violence or a tendency to loot and plunder. Therefore, 'a communal riot was a tailor-made to serve as an outlet for their social and psychological urges, as also economic needs.'[3]

According to their immediate economic needs, all classes in the society responded differently because they almost differed in their class interests. The upper class section never participated in the actual fighting, the petty-bourgeoisie often displayed caste and communal idioms and was largely benefited from it. The peasants had their own grievances and the workers lacking any political ideology could easily be exploited by the vested interests often doing the actual fighting.

First of all it is attempted to deal with the petty-bourgeois base of communal riots under conditions of relative economic stagnation. This base of communal riots may not be exaggerated and traced back to the medieval period of history. The petty-bourgeois base of communal riots is par excellence a middle class problem[4] and the emergence of middle class is consequent to the introduction of industrial capitalism.

Due to the worsening economic condition, increasing unemployment and professions overcrowded, the middle class started thinking in terms of their future programme. They faced the fear of being declassed and losing their social status. Existing opportunities and traditional sources of livelihood were fast disappearing. A certain edge and urgency was imparted to their worldly struggle to maintain their class position.[5] This frustration, a sense of social deprivation and a constant fear of loss of identity and status often created an atmosphere of violence which when triggered off by a religious issue led to communal riots. The Nawadah riot is a clear

3. Ibid., p. 66.
4. Ibid., p. 41.
5. Ibid., p. 35.

example of the petty-bourgeois base of communal riot.[6] The involvement of the lawyer in leading and attacking the Muhammadans can be marked on two grounds. Firstly to build up a political fortune in the locality by winning the hearts of the Hindu population and secondly to be beneficiaries in their professions. In this way, they could reserve the support and loyalty of the members of their respective community and thus began to be branded as 'Hindu lawyer' and 'Muslim lawyer.' Not only this, the professionals getting their positions threatened started affiliating themselves with the communal organisation of their own community. In the month of October 1939, a serious disturbance took place in Balia (Begusarai) on the occasion of the Durga Puja. The trouble originated on a very insignificant issue when a few mischief mongers among the Muslims threw stones on the crowd.[7] The Hindus retaliated by assaulting and looting some Muslim shops on the false ground that the image of Durga has been desecrated.[8] But careful perusal of the incident

6. *Political Special File No.* 110/1940 (B.S.A.). See the details of Nawadah disturbance that occurred on 28.2.1940. The District Magistrate B.N. Singh of Gaya despatched a letter to the commissioner complaining that ". . . 9 out of 17 Taziyas of town aboundened near Karbala insisting on getting across wheat fields owned by some Hindus . . ."

In the evening of 23rd February, the District Magistrate received a letter from the vice-President—'Mukhtar Association Nawadah' complaining of insult to Babu Karamchand, Mukhtar of Nawadah.

Another day, the said Mukhtar organised a meeting in the evening and the next day followed by a rumour in the whole town that 'some Muslims had deliberately insulted Karam Chand Babu' and it must be resented.

'The propaganda of insult was based on the false rumour. (From a letter of the commissioner dated 24th March 1940). On the other hand about 200 Muslims were led by some influential lawyers of the town and now came the actual incident when Karam Chand Babu led the mob ostensibly with the intention of defiling the Taziyas, *The Star of India*, dated 28th March 1940.

7. *Political Special File No.* 584/1939 (B.S.A.).
8. Ibid. See the Report of the Superintendent of Police.

suggests that the happening was pre-planned because discriminate looting of shops were made. Only a few Muslim shops were damaged and looted where Hindus and Muslims have got their shops side by side.[9] The tension existed in the village between the members of the two communities and 'this opportunity was seized on by a lawyer and President of the local Hindu Sabha, to build up a 'political position' for himself and thus instigated some 'goonda' elements to commit violence and himself has left no stone unturned in exaggerating matters between the two communities.'[10]

Thus, the crisis of colonial economy and society constantly generated two opposing sets of ideologies and political tendencies among the petty-bourgeoisie. On the one hand the slogan of 'Swaraj' appeared as immediate possibilities and on the other hand, when revolutionary change receded into the background and could no longer appeal to the petty-bourgeoisie, they shifted to short term solutions and advantages.[11] Because of the worsening economic condition in day to day life, the middle class Indians were compelled to compete with each other for the scarce opportunities and resources. There existed an intense, tough and unhealthy competition among individuals. And this competition was largely felt when an individual saw his professions overcrowded. Every available means was used in this competition and no weapon was too lowly it it could bring success within one's group. And religion proved to be the most efficient and handy tool in the hands of vested interests to realise their interests. The person engaged in a profession, in the condition of appealing economic situation believed and relied on this maxim and tried to enlist the support of his caste and community by giving sympathetic treatment to his fellow men. The riot in Bettiah that occurred on 4th August 1927 has similar story. In this riot, the partisan behaviour of a Hindu

9. Ibid. See S.P. and D.M's Report.
10. Ibid. See K.B. Sahay's note after his Ballia visit, dated 1st November 1939.
11. Bipan Chandra, op. cit., pp. 38-39.

doctor who was incharge of the Bettiah hospital, has been complained.[12] The said doctor "wrongly entered the serious and grievous wounds on the Musalmans as slight one whereas the slight on the Hindus were made grievous. . . . Some influential Hindu lawyers, and Mokhtars were seen present before the doctor."[13]

Besides, there are numerous instances of the riots taking place out of competition among the individuals for jobs, in professions, among students for prizes and scholarships. In April 1941, there was considerable tension among the students of Hindu and Muslim communities in Patna.[14] The existing tension saw its manifestation in the shouting of "Bande Matram" by some students of Patna Collegiate school. But the most ostensible issue was the distribution of prizes among the students. The crowd was seen insisting more and more on the point that 'the distribution of prizes and scholarships should be made on the population basis.'[15] It should be pointed out that an individual's failure in realising his objective was mistaken to be as due to the entrance of other caste and community. In this way, the feeling ran very high among the people of the two communities that their failure in getting services, admissions in schools and colleges was due to the coming of the rival community.[16]

The real base of Hindu-Muslim tension should be sought in economic conditions of the time. It would disappear as the conditions improve and the "agricultural, industrial and commercial development of the province affords greater

12. *Political Special File No.* 216/1917 (B.S.A.), p. 9.
13. Ibid., p. 9.
14. *Fortnightly Report to the Govt. of Bihar*, dated 5th May 1941, pp 2-3.
15. Ibid.
16. After announcement that 'backward' people will have more seats in schools and colleges and Govt. services, most of the people belonging to the 'forward' section started thinking that their present condition of the failure of achieving their objectives is due to encroachment of the people belonging to other castes. And this led to antipathy between the backward and the forward sections in present day Bihar.

opportunities for the employment of the thousands of graduates, matriculates etc. at present unable to find suitable works."[17] It leaves no doubt that the relations of the masses of the two communities do not present the same difficulties. Within the middle class section of the two communities feeling ran very high that their present conditions were due to the competition in jobs with the rival community.[18] Thus caste and communal idioms were displayed to achieve jobs, promotion or even High Court judgeship. The masses were exploited on the false promises of bringing good to the community on the one hand and the support of the masses was used as a potent weapon to make pressure on the Government on the other hand. Ali Hasan, Bar-at-Law once stated that,

> "The chief grievance of the community is that High Court bench is not represented by a Muhammadan judge. . . And the presence of a Muslim judge would create confidence in the heart of Muslim community. . . . otherwise it would be resented by the community."[19]

Thus in order to give their individual struggle a wider fighting ground, the middle classes used caste and communal identities to enhance the individual's capacity to compete through a group. This competition also took the symbolic form of competition in protecting the alleged putative rights in religious practices which led to communal riots usually organised and financed by professionals, shopkeepers and traders.[20]

It should also be noted here that only those struggles of class base did assume communal colour in which the victims and the instigators belonged to different communities. The revolt of Hindu peasants and workers against the oppression

17. *Report of the Indian Statutory Commission*, (Calcutta, 1930), Vol. III, p. 397 under the heading "Communal dissension."
18. *The Behar Herald*, dated 30th April 1927. An editorial note captioned "Communal Education."
19. *The Searchlight*, dated 14.9.1923. A letter from Ali Hasan, Bar-at-Law to the editor.
20. Bipan Chandra, op. cit., p. 37.

of Hindu landlords or moneylenders seldom took communal shape. The socio-economic struggles were not of course, always distorted into communal channels. The peasants and workers and the radical intelligentsia did create powerful secular class movements and organisations after 1918.[21] But in most of the cases, the struggle led by the peasants and workers of one community against the oppression of landlords, moneylanders or the mill-owner belonging to other, the fight at once was magnified into a Hindu-Muslim fight.[22] To-day the rich peasant capitalist farmer's conflict with the agricultural labourer is sought to be given a caste form. The rich peasants do so to mobilise the poor and middle peasants of their own castes behind themselves. Certain radical sounding political leaders do so to hide the increasing class differentiation within the ranks of the lower castes and thus to use their social and economic oppression for their own class ends.

Another petty-bourgeoisie base of communal riots may be sought in the tensions ensuing out of competition in trade and business. An individual belonging to a particular community engaged in trading and business activities could display communal idioms only at a time when his interests were largely jeopardised by the entrance of other traders and businessmen. Unfortunately, this aspect of communal problem has not been studied yet.

A struggle within an exploiting class taking some other guise is also a well known social phenomenon, especially under conditions of economic underdevelopment and stagnation. This is particularly so where new entrants fight against the older, entrenched persons for control over non-expanding or stagnant economic opportunities. In this struggle both the

21. In modern India most of the peasant struggles from the Indigo Rebellion and Pabna agrarian unrest to present movements in U.P. and the early 1920s and 1930s in Bihar, Tebhaga struggle in Bengal took secular forms. See Bipan Chandra, op. cit., p. 61.
22. *The Behar Herald*, Sept. 19, 1925. The address note of Nilkantha Chatterjee, the Chairman of the Reception Committee in 16th Bihar Provincial Conference.

new-entrants and the entrenched persons find it necessary to form some groupings so that wider social and political forces can be mobilised in their support. Such groupings can take many forms, the communal form being one of them. The disturbance that occurred at Bettiah on 4th August 1927 on the occasion of 'Jhanda procession' had similar base of communal riot. Though the immediate cause of the trouble appeared to be the religious but the main problem centred round land and the rivalry ensuing out of the competition in trade.[23] The Muslims in Bettiah for the last few years have been taking interest in trade and shoping which were previously dominated by Hindus.[24] The immediate cause of the conflict may be traced back to the murder of a Muslim boy 'who got settlement of some land in the 'Kachhary' to open a shop in spite of the objections made by Hindu middlemen.'[25]

For having a clear understanding of communal conflict, it is also necessary to understand some local characteristics of a communal situation. Most of the riots tend to occur in medium sized towns because in such towns petty-bourgeois elements who are usually quite conservative and often tend to be communal predominate. Among these medium sized towns those with larger proportions of Muslim population, fifty per cent are more riot prone. (The idea has been formed during the course of investigation of several riots that occur in these areas). The tendency to be riot prone gets further intensified if there exists, among Muslims in the town, an entrepreneurial class competing with, and challenging the monopoly of the Hindu businessmen or vice versa. A riot of this nature took place at Sahokhar in Patna district on 2nd May 1928.[26] It was the period of economic crisis and its effects were largely felt in almost every branch of economic structure. When the rival merchants promoted the view that

23. *Political Special File No.* 216/1927 (B.S.A.), pp. 32-33.
24. Ibid.
25. Ibid.
26. *Political Special File No.* 92/1928 (B.S.A.). After investigation the subinspector states that 'the incident was premeditated.' The initiative was taken by Ram Lal Teli who had a 'biri' shop.

customers should patronise shopkeepers of their own religion. In this way, the organised communal riots were also financed by rival merchants who would raise funds to hire the lumpen and goonda elements to do the actual fighting.[27]

The sense of economic insecurity resulted in strained social relations leading to boycott of one community by the other. These tendencies also accelerated the pace of communal violence. Such incident of 'boycott and cessation' of social relations has seen at Shahabad in the year 1925.[28] To ease social tension. secret meetings by the leading members of the two communit es were held and resolutions were made to this effects.[29] The resolution on the Muhammadan side read as, 'The Muhammadans should in future take up the profession of 'palanquin' bearers in place of Hindus' and Muhammadans should prepare sweets and open shops which was the monopoly of Hindu Halwai.' On the other hand, Hindus insisted on 'taking up the trade of meat selling once dominated by the Muslim butchers' and the Hindu low caste people would sell vegetables to the public instead of employing Muslim middlemed. The members of both the communities negotiated and no any trouble did take place.[30]

Thus, communal politics as also communal riots often disguised commercial rivalry among merchants and shopkeepers. This factor became quite important during the great depression from 1929 to 1939 and during the second world war. These socio-economic tensions resulted in the abrogation of law and order followed by mass murder and looting. At Champanagar, a suburb of Bhagalpur on 24th January 1940, Muhammadan mobs consisting mainly of 'momins' attacked and looted the Hindu shops of 'Tatis.' The motive for the

27. Bipan Chandra, op. cit., p. 70.
28. *Political Special File No.* 271/1925 (B.S.A.). Extract from the confidential diary of S.P. Shahabad for the week ending August 17, 1925.
29. Ibid.
30. *Political Special File No.* 271/1925 (B.S.A.).

attack was the ill-feeling arising out of the trade rivalry among them as boththe Tantis and Momins were weavers.[31]

In post-independence India, this base of communal riots have assumed large proportions. Keeping the characteristics in mind one can easily understand why the towns like Moradabad, Aligarh, Meerut, Jamshedpur, Benaras and Bhiwindi are frequent scenes of communal eruptions. The Moradabad riot of 1980 has a obviously petty-bourgeois base. Muslims in Moradabad had traditionally been artisans making brassware vessels. *Punjabis had the monopoly* of trade in brassware and Muslims entering this field disturbed them. *And this threat to trading interests* resulted in communal riot.[32]

Throughout the twentieth century, there existed extremely poor economic opportunities and increasing unemployment due to the absence of modern industries and because of shrinking Government expenditure. The position of the lower middle class worsened all the more because of their double way exploitation by the indigenous merchants, moneylenders and capitalists. In other words, the lower middle class were increasingly placed in a position of economic misery and lack of opportunity. Peasants, who had no any other opportunity apart from land, faced with fixed debt charges and the rate of revenue demands became intolerable.[33]

Thus, in this crisis-ridden economy apart from middle and lower middle classes, the peasants *too could fall prey* to respond to the communal problem. The disputes regarding the possession and use of lands gave a new lease of life to rural violence. It should be made here clear that, in the tensions centering round lands, mostly lower caste people like

31. *Fortnightly Report, Govt. of Bihar*, dated 3rd Feb , 1940, p. 3.
32. I have presented a paper to the *Indian History Congress* (Burdwan, 1983) entitled 'Socio-economic base of communal riots in India: A brief survey' (1890-1980), p 435.
33. M.K. Gandhi, *Young India*, dated 28th May 1930.

Mahtos, Kurmis, Goalas and Koeris participated who fought for the betterment of their existing conditions.[34] The involvement and direct connection between upper caste people and communal riots has rarely been noticed. In most of the cases, these people played the role of instigators because most of them were land holding people.[35] A communal riot due to the conflict over a piece of land was reported from Nawadih Baijanathpur (Deoghar), but soon after it was given communal colour.[36]

On 17th September 1928, a communal riot occurred at Karanmeya village (Bettiah). The trouble arose out of a land owned by a Hindu and the Muslims persuaded to use it as a burial ground.[37] Previously Hindus and Muslims at the village lived amicably and participated in the functions organised by one another. The crisis of land was increasingly becoming acute due to the problem of unemployment in Government services on the one hand and on the other hand, the growing population of the country was a great burden especially for those who had no other opportunities other than the land. In this circumstance competition for control over 'Parati' and 'Jagir' lands started further embittering social relation.

34. Sumit Sarkar, op. cit., pp. 54-57.

35. In Bihar the social composition of the Zamindars i.e. land holding classes was predominantly Bhumihar with small numbers of Kayasthas, Muslims, Rajputs and Brahmins. See, Water Hauser's dissertation submitted for Ph.D. in Chicago University, *The Provincial Kisan Sahha 1929-1942 ; A Study of Indian Peasant Movement*, (Chicago, 1961), p. 13.

36. *Political Special File No.* 106/1928 (B.S.A.). 'Hemat Ali who was prosecuted in this case stated that some Hindus of the village destroyed the mosque.' But the report from the D.I.G., C.I D. dated 11th May 1928 stated that 'Hemat Ali had a piece of land from a Hindu and was building a house. The land was given without the previous knowledge of other shareholders, who objected and resisted the construction. Thereupon, Hemat Ali, 'to get support of his community pretended that a mosque had been demolished by a Hindu.'

37. *Political Special File No.* 111/1928 (B.S.A.).

On 23rd October 1928, a certain section of the two communities came at daggers drawn 'due to the construction of a school by the Muslim of eight families on a Jagirland.'[38] But soon they were forbidden by some Hindus under the instigation of the 'Gomastha' of the Hathwa Raj. To save the land, the Muslims pretended that their houses were looted. burnt and damaged by the Hindus.[39] It is to be pointed out that the tension between the two communities existed apart from any religious issue. The problem centred round land. But immediately it was magnified into a communal problem.

Communal tactics and jargons were more often displayed by the vested interests to conceal the real nature of the struggle and also to provide wider fighting ground to their individual problems. A fight of Muslim agriculturists against the oppression of Hindu landlord in the village of Harnawali district (Lahore) assumed communal colour. The main fight centred round the possession of land.[40] As the Hindu landlord and some of his men came to attack debtor's land, but were opposed by a party of Muslim cultivators. But the conflict was seen as a Hindu attack on the Muslim community.[41] Such absentee landlords often brought much more misery to the poor agriculturists. But the fight of purely class base was given shape of a communal tussle.

In large parts of Bengal and Bihar, the tenants and debtors were mostly Muslims while the Zamindars and moneylenders were largely upper caste Hindus. Morover, the mostly absentee or non-managing Zaminders managed their estates through 'naibs' or agents who were largely Hindus even in the case of Muslim Zamindars. The ryots often felt direct oppression in the person of these Hindu naibs.[42] The problem

38. *Ibid., Memo No. 781-84 C.*
39. Ibid.
40. *The Behar Herald*, dated 29th September 1934. An editorial note entitled 'Hindus Clash with Musalmans'.
41. Ibid.
42. See an article "Communal Riots in Bengal 1930-31" by Tanik Sarkar in M Hasan, *Communal and Pan-Islamic Trends in Colonial India* (ed), (Delhi, 1981), p. 304.

of Muslim tenants· or debtors were, of course, not peculiarly Muslim. The Hindu tenants or debtors suffered no less than the Muslims from rack-renting, high rates of interests and other forms of agrarian. Thus. Tanik Sarkar writes oppression that:

> "What were fundamentally agrarian jacqueries or the fury of the urban poor against a social system reinforced by an alien imperialism turned into communal fighting due to imperfect politicisation.[43]

In worse economic condition, rural communal conflict often disguised a struggle over appropriation of communal land or between cattle owning peasant and butchers, who encouraged cattle theft. During 1930s dacoities were a major problem in Patna and Gaya districts.[44] Due to these negative developments there was acute rural tension. The gangsters and noted criminals were at times patronised by the landlord because these anti-social elements often did come in direct tussle with the people and, therefore, weakened class conflict. These goonda elements acted on the support of the members of their respective communities because they appeared to be the champions of Hindus or Muslims. Thus, class cleavage became sharper than ever and communal antagonism also accelerated its pace. The riot that occurred at Kairabad village in Bihar subdivision in 1932 got its genesis after the harvesting of paddy crops by some badly reputed persons of the Goala community from the lands owned by a Muslim peasant at the instigation of a local Zamindar.[45]

Besides, there are numerous instances of communal riots arising out of the 'collection of funds' by some individuals of a community from others. When one failed in realising it, appealed to the masses on the false plea that the members of the rival community have malafide intentions against their religion. The riot of this nature did take place at the village

43. Ibid.
44. *Political Special File No.* 400/1947 (B.S.A.).
45. *Political Special File No.* 3011/1932 (B.S.A.). See the report by the D.S.P.

Bedaul Amidha in Darbhanga in October 1928.[46] The genesis of the trouble may be sought in the acts of some local goalas who made a vow that if the Hathia rainfall arrived in time to save their crops, they would go on a begging expedition to collect funds to offer Puja to Lord Mahadeo. Accordingly they took out a begging procession with musical accomplishments and the Muslims opposed the music.[47] It should be concluded after the perusal of the whole incident that the Muslims objected when Hindus started exacting money from the Muslims [48] And soon the influential leaders among the Hindus brought the situation in the way the Muslim were opposing the Puja celebrations.

Therefore, it would be quite misleading and rather unsociological to treat communal riots as a religious conflict between the two communities. Behind communal riots religion had never been the real issue but such riots add to the popularity of one or other communal party or group and strengthens the economic interests in the field of trade, profession, money-lending etc.[49]

As pointed out above, economic competition often results in communal conflict. All it indicates is that in a backward capitalist economy and in a country like India with its multicaste and multicommunal socio-economic formations, straight class conflict is bound to be replaced by caste-class and community-class conflict, sometimes class factor becoming predominant and at times caste or community factor becoming predominant. In addition to class conflict the complexities and uniqueness of Indian situation is also reflected through caste and communal conflict.

Now the question arises, what was the configuration of rural forces that helped communal polarisation? In most

46. *Political Special File No*. 111/1928.
47. Ibid.
48. Ibid. Confidential diary report of the S.P. Darbhanga dated 7th October 1928.
49. S.M. Chand, *National Leaders on Communalism*, (Jaipur, 1985), p. 136.

parts of Bengal and Bihar, landlords, traders and mahajans were overwhelmingly Hindu. Partly because of a religious taboo on usury, Muslims generally kept out of moneylending activities which were monopolised by Bengali 'Sahas' and Bihari 'banias' and more recently of Marwaris.[50] The pattern of rioting, the main targets, the chief participants, and the aims of rioters reveal that these were either rural or urban social protests behind the facade of Hindu or Muslim attack. In most of the cases, we see that temples and mosques were seldom attacked, domestic shrines were rarely desecrated and only houses along with shops, Godowns and markets that were seen as symbols of wealth and ostentation were attacked. In this way, the propertied class were at more disadvantage. Such a definitely class base selection of targets reminds us of the Gordon riot of 1780 in London when anti Catholic rioters concentrated only on houses of rich Catholics.[51]

Yet outbrack of the second world war resulted in high prices, acute poverty and mass upsurge against exploitation. The Bihar riots in the wake of observance of 'Noakhali day' on 25th October 1947 revealed yet another pattern, more difficult to explain : a mass upsurge of Hindu peasants against Muslims, resulting in massacre far more terrible really than Noakhali.[52] A horrified and bewildered Nehru reported that "A madness has seized the people in what was an old Congress stronghold," he suspected some landlord instigation to divert the attention of their tenantry from agrarian problems.[53] Of course, the riots that did take place in Bihar in October-November had strong class content. At several places only rich and affluent Muslims were attacked. The riot of 25th October 1947 which resulted in large massacre at Singha Chouri (Muzaffarpur), was also selection based attack. Poor Muslims were given shelter by the poor 'Khatwar' almost all of whom

50. M. Hasan, op. cit., p. 311.
51. George Rude, *Crowds in History 1790-1848* (New York, 1964) Chapter VII, p. 308,
52. Sumit Sarkar, op. cit., p. 433.
53. Ibid. Also see S.M. Chand, op. cit., p. 63.

worked as labourers. The attack was made by poor Hindus on a rich Muslim who was affluent and had a cultivation of about 40 bighas of land.[54] It has also been reported that the attacks were mainly planned by those persons who took loans from the rich Muslims of the village.

In brief it should be concluded that the use of communal symbols, haphazard urbanisation, increasing religiosity, fierce competition in trade and for jobs, communalised politics, non-functioning of colonial institutions, displacement and non-absorption of workers and clustering of religious and caste groups provide sufficient conditions for communal riots. The underdeveloped colonial economy has failed to solve the basic problems of poverty, unemployment and inequality which breed frustration and generates unhealthy competition for the inadequate social and economic opportunities. Jawahar Lal Nehru in the 1930s endeavoured to seek connections between the various communal demands and the masses. He loudly remarked,

> "At the most the communal problems deal with some jobs for a few of the unemployed intellectuals. Heated arguments take place about seats in councils and separate and joint electorates can affect or interest only a few.…Is the starving peasant likely to be interested in this when hunger gnaws his stomach? The communal leaders always try to divert attention of the people to entirely unreal, and from the masses point of view, trivial matters."[55]

Munshi Prem Chand, a great story writer of the 20th century, having argued that the British were solely responsible for communal division, he contended that there was no basic difference between Muslim and Hindu cultures. In food and dress habits, he wrote Hindus and Muslims of a particular

54. *Political Special File No.* 2665/1947 (B.S.A.), p. 54. The Report of the Commissioner after his visit at Singha Chouri on 27.10 47.
55. Moin Shakir, 'Politics of Minorities,' quoted in A.B. Shah's article "What Als aur Muslims" in *The Mirror*, December 1980, p. 18.

region were similar. Even the Hindi-Urdu controversy was not the cause of division between the two communities for this was limited to the educated few. Prem Chand did not find it difficult to assert 'that real war of tomorrow would be economic.'[56]

He seems to have found in the idea of economic conflict a possible way out of the communal tangle. "The source of communal conflict lay in the differences among the educated with regard to their rights and interests." He does not restrict it to the middle classes alone but further remarks that communal conflict is basically "the fight between two beggars for a single piece of bread".[57]

The problem did not end merely with the entry into a job, profession or trade, for then came the life long individual quest and competition for promotion, betterment and success. Every available means was adopted in this matter if it could bring success within one's group.[58] But to give their struggle a wider fighting ground the vested interest used other group identities such as caste, province, region and religion to enhance the individual's capacity to compete through a group,[59]

In this way, communal politics and also the communal riots often distorted or misinterpreted social tension and class conflict between the exploiters and the exploited into communal conflict. Popular discontent was usually due to non-religious and non-communal factors. But under the backward social and economic conditions, it found a distorted expression in communal tension. Under the pressure of communal propaganda the masses are unable to locate the real causes of their exploitation, suffering and oppression and thus class oppression was seen to be the communal oppression.[60]

56. Amrita Ray, *Vividh Prasang* (Hindi) edited, (Allahabad, 1975), Vol. II, pp. 378-79.
57. Ibid., pp. 393 and 111.
58. Bipan Chandra, op. cit., p. 35.
59. Ibid., p. 37.
60. C.G. Shah, *Marxism Gandhism Stalinism*, (Bombay, 1963), p. 185. We may also note that the mobilisation of the peasantry around religious symbols, slogans and ideologies in its struggle against agrarian oppression is a common occurrence in pre-modern societies.

It is nevertheless, extraordinary how the bourgeois both among the Hindu and the Muslims, succeed in the sacred name of religion; in getting mass sympathy and support for programmes and demands which had absolutely to do with the masses or even the lower middle class. Every one of the communal demands which had absolutely nothing to do with the masses or even the lower middle class. Everyone of the communal demands put forward by any communal group is, in the final analysis, a demand for jobs, and these jobs could only go to a handful of the upper middle class for special and additional seats in the legislatures, as symbolising political powers, but this too is looked from chiefly as the power to exercise patronage. These narrow political demands, benefiting at the most a small number of the upper middle classes, and often creating barriers in the way of national unity and progress were clearly made to appear the demands of the masses of that particular religious group.

In this way political reactionaries came back to the political field in the guise of communal leaders and the real explanation of the various steps they took was not so much their communal bias as their desire to obstruct political advance. Nehru saw the support that the Zamindars, princes and capitalists were giving to the communal organisations. All social and reactionary elements have found in communal organisations the only means of keeping their vested interests. According to Nehru,

> "These vested interests wanted to prevent common people from solving their problems, emancipating themselves from the curse of poverty and raising their standard of living. And thus behind the facade of religion, vested interests, particularly the zamindars and the capitalists were fighting against the economic policies of the progressive Governments at the Centre and the Provinces."[61]

61. S.M. Chand, op. cit., p. 63.

Nehru further remarks that the ostrich like policy of the communalists of ignoring the real issue is bound to end in disaster.' It is, therefore, obvious that the communal problem is basically embedded in the roots of economy and to make endeavour to solve it on religious and social plane is quite misleading. Every society from slave owing to the present capitalist society has a characteristic tendency of division apart from class line along caste and communal line. This division has ever been exploited by the ruling party to check the political consciousness along class line among the masses. Their popular resentment against oppression is soon channelised into caste and communal conflict and thus class base remains rather obscure in these socio-economic conditions. To say the least, communal riots are in fact the perverted form of class struggle.

5

Social Classes and Communal Problem

Communal riots cannot be understood in isolation from a comprehension of the level of operation of communal ideology. The notion that communal riots have their own dynamism and can be tackled independent of the various complex of social phenomena is not only partial but counter-productive. Without having a clear understanding of the character and the role played by the persons belonging to different classes in the society it would be quite misleading to develop the theory of communal riots. Communal riots cannot be explained by giving only a mono-casual explanation which is neither adequate nor desirable. The anti-social elements are merely the instruments used to achieve ends set by vested interests. Individuals or groups may use this riff-raff and may themselves actively participate in communal riots. The other participants in communal violence as a class can be categorised as: Instigators, Participant-Instigators, Active participants and Accidental beneficiaries.

Instigators are those who hope to gain or do gain directly through the propagation of communal ideology and by engineering riots. These instigators are mainly drawn from amongst industrialists, traders, landlords and political and religious leaders and bureaucrats who have their own vested class interests. In this chapter it is proposed to discuss their roles separately.

During the last two decades of the nineteenth century, the cow-protection movement swept Northern India. Though the movement started to preserve bovine population for economic reasons. But soon the movement began to take roots and it acquired social, political and above all religious dimensions.[1] The movement soon acquired religious patronage and unfortunately fell into the hands of the vested interests. For them, religion had become the most handy instrument to realise their political ambitions and religious leaders i.e. 'pandits' and 'purohits' became the sole agents. The communalists both among the Hindus and the Muslims made best of the issue to grind their political axes. These developments resulted in social tension at the mass level and rather widened the gulf existing between the Hindus and the Muslims. The communal antagonism at times suited the colonial Government but when the movement resulted in large scale riots and created law and order problem it became a matter of serious concern for the Government.[2]

The main agencies for the spread of cow-protection movement were the 'Gorakshini Sabhas' which were well organised at all India plane, and resorted to tactics, jargons which appealed to all sections of Hindus in the society. This movement was started as an 'organised and planned movement by the Arya Samaj' and was joined gradually by the 'Dharam Sabhas' or orthodox Hindu elements in the society.[3]

In order to attract large numbers the Sabhas circulated 'Dharampatras' warning the people that if a Hindu did not

1. S.A.A. Tirmizi, "The Cow Protection Movement and mass mobilisation in Northern India 1882-93", *Proceeding of the Indian History Congress* (Waltair, 1979), p. 575.
2. Ibid.
3. L.S.S. O'Malley, *Bengal District Gazetteer: Muzaffarpur*, (Calcutta, 1907), pp. 32-33.

abide by the rules of the Sabhas, it will be considered sin on the part of Hinduism and the man will be considered born of butchers. In addition to it, ploughman's *begging* movement was started to keep the cow protectian agitation afloat.[4] Besides, rules and regulations were established for the people adhering to these ideals. If one dared to go against these norms, Brahmanas, purohit or kinsman often declined to eat at his house. "No Chamar, Lohar or Washerman were allowed to work for such persons. The Sabha was authorised to prevent even the marriage of his children.[5]

As a matter of fact, these Sabhas constituted themselves into tribunal trying the offenders against the movement. The chief weapon in the hands of the Sabhas was the power of outcasting, imposing religious penalties and fine. Therefore, the fear of social boycott forced the people to adhere to these ideals.

The Gorakshanists on many occasions played on the fears of the people by telling them that if they did not care for the mother 'cow' they will die issueless and as a leper. The curse of cow-killing will fall on their property, service and offsprings.[6] It has already been discussed in Chapter III.

In order to mobilise public opinion the cow protectionist tried to whip up communal and religious passions. The lecturers or the paid agents of the societies were asked to lecture on the past glories of Hinduism when no cow-slaughter used to take place. Later on, the communalists played on this point and harped loudly that no slaughter did take

4. Ibid.
5. S.A.A. Tirmizi, op. cit., p. 576.
6. 'It was propagated that Lord Mahadeo had imposed upon the people to expiate the sin committed by agricultural community in overworking their cattle.'
L.S.S. O'Malley, *District Gazetteer: Muzaffarpur*, (Calcutta, 1907), p. 33.

place in ancient India.[7] Communal sentiments were aroused through press, provocative tracts and plays.

The cow protection societies had a regular hierarchy of officials consisting of Dharam Sabhapati, Sabhapati, General Secretaries and other officials like treasurers etc. The meetings were conducted by prior notices through circulars at times by leading 'fakir' or 'sannayasins' requesting persons who received the circular and pass it on to other people.[8]

Because of these well organised propaganda the movement gained wide support. Many a time the movement created antagonism between Hindus and Muslims. It was because Hindus involved in provocative rescue of cattle also demanded agreements or 'Iqrarnama' from the Muhammadans to the extent that they would not indulge in cow-slaughter. The Hindus also threatened the Muslims that if they did not abide by the agreement then they would be plundered and boycotted by the Hindus. Sometimes, the Muslims were forcibly prevented from using village wells and were treated untouchables and 'Malechchas.'[9] These repeated insistence on these lines generated a sense of reaction among the Muslims and the vested interest among them made slaughter Islamic in the eyes of Muslim masses.

At times, the Hindu landlords exploited the communal sentiments and ejected the Muslim tenantry. The landlords among the Hindus and the Muslims promoted obscurantism and patronised such movements because of its capacity to distort popular struggles, to prevent the masses from understanding the social and economic factors responsible for their

7. 'Hinduism owes much to the vedas and the 'Rig veda' itself mentions cow slaughter where the guests were called goghan (one who feds on beef)'.

   R.S. Sharma, *Ancient India*, (Delhi, 1977), pp. 52-55.

8. *Political Special File No.* 1346/1916 (B.S.A.). In a meeting organised by Hindu ecclesiastics, several 'patias' were distributed that read as follows :

   "सभी हिन्दुओं से अर्ज है कि पत्र पढ़कर 10 पत्र को दस गाँव में भेज दें, नहीं तो 10 गो-वध करने का दोष होगा। आगे यह प्रार्थना किया जाता है कि आप सभी ऐसा काम करें जिससे सनातन धर्म को उपकार होगा।"

9. L.S.S. O'Malley, *District Gazetteer*, *Saran*, (Calcutta, 1908), pp, 39-41.

social condition and to turn them away from their real national and socio-economic interests and issues and mass movements around them.[10] Dne to these sectional interests. the landlords nourished and gave moral and material assistance to these religious organisations. In U.P. the Muslims school master addressed the meeting to throw light on the necessity to protect cows. But soon its leadership passed into the hands of Hindu landlords. In April 1893 several religious mendicants entered in several districts of Bihar and preached the well known doctrine of the Gorakshini Society.[11] Not only largely attended meetings were held in market towns, but in many villages community officers were appointed to this purpose. Everywhere subscription for the preservation of cattle were collected from all classes of Hindus.[12] In the meantime however secret letters were handed from village to village purporting to come from the Pundits of Benaras. Acting on the instructions contained in these letters, the Hindus proceeded to persecute the Mohammadans. They refused to allow them to draw water from the village wells, where from time immemorial the Muslims had peacefully done so side by side with the Hindus.[13]

Soon the society fell into the trap of Hindu landlords in Bihar. The Maharaja of Darbhanga, his cousins Durga Dutt Singh and Hakhdhari Singh, his employees and other landlords of Bettiah, Tikari were its leaders. Its literature was printed in the Raj Press, Darbhanga.[14] These landlords in collaboration with imperialists in their respective class interests set in motion the process of disintegration and disunity. The cousins of Maharaja of Darbhanga were instrumental in opening the branch of Gorakshini Sabha at Sitamarhi.[15] At Katia Taur (Aurangabad) on the 25th March

10. Bipan Chandra, *Communalism in Modern India*, p. 79.
11. L.S.S. O'Malley, *District Gazetteer, Saran*, (Calcutta, 1908), pp. 39-41.
12. Ibid.
13. Ibid.
14. V.C P. Choudhary, *Communalism Versus Secularism*, p. 22.
15. Ibid.

1893, the Muslims and a constable were attacked under the leadership of a dependent of the Maharaja of Deo.[16]

Since then communal riots have started taking place out of the rescue of cattle by the Hindus. The rescue of cattle was not limited to Muslim butchers alone but there were also organised rescue from cantonment areas and the cattle meant for the armies.[17] Another incident of this type came to light from Arwal (Jehanabad) when some commissariat agents were taking 34 head of cattle from a fair to the Dinapore cantonment, when they were set upon a body of Hindus who forcibly carried off the cattle.[18] Thus, communal sentiments enabled the vested groups to disguise their own privileged sectional economic and political interests in the garb of communal ideology and religious identity and instead to secure for their interests not only a moral and ideological cover but also popular mass support, inspired by religious passions. In 1920s the Gorakshini Sabha gained active support from the Marwaris and other members of the merchant class who displayed more favour than most of their co-religionists towards the object of Hindu veneration.[19]

The use of symbols and slogans that had very little indeed to do with the communal issues at stake, and the mobilisation of support along lines of kind and caste, there are some of the features that stand out from the evidence relating to the riots that broke out on the occasion of the Bakr-Id of 1917 and 1918 in Patna, Gaya and Shahabad. The evidence here is more confusing, but it appears that the local Hindus who were the aggressors had a planned and a limited demonstration to protest against, and if possible prevent the

16. *Political Police Proceeding* (1891-95). p. 6
17. Ibid., p. 5. 'One Lotun Kasai was taking nine head of cattle on 23rd Nov. 1893 to the Sonepur fair for the commissariat department, when he came near Rajapur village, a large number of villagers attacked him and carried off the cattle.'
18. *Political Police Proceeding* (1891-95), p. 5.
19. L.S.S. O'Malley, *Bihar and Orissa District Gazetteer, Saran* (Calcutta, 1924), p. 59.

performance of 'Qurbani' in the village Ibrahimpur (Shahabad).[20]

The 1917 riots were the culmination of a recrudescence in cow-protection activities after 1910. In the Patna division, this had synchronised with the Gwala movement' who were in constant fight against the members of the upper castes. They were fighting for their social status and they followed the social customs and taboos of the upper caste Hindus in the process of Sankritisation.[21] In this fight for existence, they were made to think that if they did lend their whole-hearted support to the socio-religious movements, they will be able to enjoy upper cast status and privileges in the society. Thus, later on the prevention of cow-slaughter became a major object of the Gwalas and the movement gained its active support from the upper caste people i.e. Rajputs, Bhumihars, Kayasthas and Marwaris.[22] Previously, the Gorakshini Sabha and such other organisations were promoted and led by the upper caste people in the society. More often they were the leaders in mobilising the people to prevent slaughter. In 1911, crowds of Gwalas and Bhumihars collected and prevented the sacrifices at several places in Patna district. In 1915, what was described as a "large armed Rajput mob" was active towards the same in Kanchanpur and Barawan villages in Fatwa thana in Patna district.[23]

The frequency of riots increased during the 1920s and every province was badly affected. From this period, on a new cause namely religious conversion came to be added to the existing sources of conflict. New militant organisations of Hindus, 'Suddhi' and 'Sangathan' launched by the Arya

20. Gyanendra Pandey's "Sectarian and other solidarities: some observations on commuual mobilisation in Modern India" in *Proceeding of the Indian History Congress*, (Waltair, 1979), p 625.
21. Sumit Sarkar, op. cit , p. 158.
22. P. Robbert's "Officials and non-officials as leaders in popular agitation : Shahabad 1917 and conspiracies" in B.N. Pandey, *Leadership in South Asia* (ed), (Delhi, 1977), p. 182.
23. *Political Special File No.* 1165/1916 (B.S.A.). Extract from the fortnightly confidential report.

Samaj and 'Tanjeem' and 'Tabligh' among the Muslims added to the such of communal violence.[24]

It is not intended here to stimatise Arya Samaj. If any comment is necessary it is that the Suddhi movement was also not unprovoked. In all probability it was a Hindu reaction to the superior' powers of mobilisation demonstrated by the Muslims during the Khilafat movement. Mr. Fazlur Rehman, Chairman of the local board addressed a meeting on the 30th June 1933 and remarked, "... During Khilafat and non-cooperation movements both Hindus and Muslims worked unitedly but all of a sudden Suddhi movement of the Hindu Mahasabha spoiled everything and India was again plunged into the feuds of communalism."[25]

The Arya Samajists were no doubt working under the noble impulses of bring socio-religious reforms within Hinduism. This organisation undoubtedly lessened caste rigidities, condemned flesh eating and drinking. It encouraged social reforms like widow remarriage but from the very beginning the movement started attacking and counter-attacking other religious organisations of the other community. In processions, the Arya Samajists sang songs against other religious groups resulting in arousing the hostility of other communities.[26]

Like Arya Samaj, several socio-religious organisations sprang up in the Muslim community too, 'Anjuman Islamia' and Tanjeem Committee being some of them.[27] These organisations acted on the sole intention of counteracting Arya Samaj and 'Sanatan Dharma.' Gnce a Muslim ecclesiastic on behalf of the Anjuman Hidyatul Islam of Delhi, visited Patna City and delivered lectures at several places. In

24. *Bihar and Orissa Police Abstract of Intelligence* 1917, para. 107, p. 45.
25. *Political Special File No.* 169/1933 (B.S.A.). Proceedings of the Provincial Muslim Conference held at Kishanganj, Purnia.
26. *Bihar and Orissa Police Abstract of Intelligence 1912*, p. 2.
27. *Political Special File No.* 217/1933 (B.S.A.).

the course of his speech, he pointed out certain defects in the Arya Samaj creed but he was strongly resisted by an Arya Samajist.[28] Later on, some Arya Samajists coming from Agra gave lectures on the 'Koran' and Islamic religion.[29] These lectures created a sort of ill-feeling and uneasiness in the minds of the people which was likely to result in breach of peace at several places.[30]

Due to these developments, the relationship between the Hindus and the Muslims in Bihar were severely strained during the year 1923 despite the efforts of political leaders to encourage mutual forbearance and unity.[31] The main source of dissension was the conversion of Musalman Rajputs to the Arya Samaj creed in the province, and fears were entertained by the more orthodox Muhammadans that the movement would spread to the several parts of the province.[32] To combat this attack on their faith, funds were collected and Muhammadan preachers were despatched to oppose the Hindu's missionaries' actions which in turn provoked counter propaganda from Hindus and mutual recriminations resulted in Shahabad, Saran, Muzaffarpur, Monghyr, and Patna.[33] Mr. Mujibur Rehman in a secret meeting held at Calcutta in 1929 loudly lamented saying that "we should check the progress of suddhi" and further spoke encouraging the people of his community that "I am not going to discourage you to raise cry against sudhi.[34]

These developments brought a new source of misery to the people. From now onward on a new cause 'music before mosque' much fighting did take place between the two communities. All mutual relations were snapped following

28. *Bihar and Orissa Police Abstract of Intelligence* 1912, para. 107, p. 45.
29. Ibid.
30. Ibid.
31. *Administrative Reports to the Govt. of Bihar & Orissa* (1923-24), p. 6.
32. Ibid.
33. Ibid.
34. *Political Special File No.* 182/1933 (B.S.A.).

the arousal of religious hostility of the two communities. The common form of provocation was the deliberate defilement of temples and mosques. The activities of the Arya Samajists were doubtful and they did play very significant role in provocation.[35] In December 1926, the murder of Swami Shradhanand, a popular Arya Samajist caused a sensation in the tension prone areas of Bihar and in other parts of the country also. The Hindus in most of the towns observed 'hartals' in his memory and there was a good deal of excited oratory resulting in bitter feeling.[36]

The murder of Swami Shradhanand at Delhi caused a certain amount of anti-Muslim feeling in Bihar. Now the Arya Samajists who once worked under the noble ideas of social transformation resorted to open violence and provided moral and material assistance to the elements who spread anti-Muslim rumour among the people. The communal riot that took place in Bettiah on 30th May 1928 was started by a well known Arya Samajist of the area.[37]

In August 1927, a very serious riot occurred in the Champaran district. The occasion of the rioting was Mahabiridal procession, a Hindu festival primarily of minor importance but in the last few years organised on a large scale to compensate low caste Hindus for the absence from Muharram which the Arya Samajists had imposed upon them.[38]

The emergence of Arya Samaj in the recent years is an interesting phenomenon. Its aggressive campaign on the question of conversion had dangerous communal potentialities

35 *Administrative Report to the Govt. of Bihar and Orissa* (1926-27), pp. 5-7.

36. Ibid.

37. *Political Special File No.* 111/1928 (B S.A.). 'The riot was engineered by Kamalanand Tiwary and Ramanand Sonar, well known Arya Samajists, of the town in collaboration with some school students.'

38. *Report of the Indian Statutory Commission* (Calcutta, 1930), Vol. III, Section VI, p. 573.

and led to several bloody riots in the province. Conversion itself has been motivated by socio-economic factors rather than religious preference or theological involvement. The Harijans who were mercilessly exploited by the upper caste Hindus, converted themselves to Islam or Christianity because Islam seldom accepted untouchability.[39]

Many a time the question of conversion resulted in communal riot, on the problem of conversion a serious riot did take place in Bettiah on 4th August 1927.[40] In Bettiah subdivision there lived a Musalman sect called 'Gaddi', 25,000 in population. They were quite illiterate and most of their customs resembled those of the Hindus. The Arya Samajists were trying to convert them to Hinduism.[41] When the Hindu Sabha was founded here and the Congressmen joined it, they resented the Muslim activities among the Gaddis and all the leading Hindus attempted to spread the Suddhi and Sangathan movement in the area.[42] On 19th June 1927 a grand meeting was held at Patjirwa thana (Bettiah) with a view to convert the Gaddis to Hinduism. But the very plan proved abortive. The Hindus present there being hopeless reapproached the local Hindus provoking that the Hindus present there had been insulted. In the same way, another meeting on 3rd July 1927 was arranged at Siswa thana in Jogpatti.[43] The Gaddis refused to attend this meeting but the local Zamindars went on trying to bring the Gaddis to the meeting with their 'Chaparasis.' But again the meeting resulted in utter hopelessness. The tension persisted on this point and did find its expression in the breach of peace by a planned attack made on the Ramnaomi day.[44]

The initiatives regarding conversion were taken primarily by the landlords and active support was extended

39. *The Behar Herald*, dated 29th February 1936. Text of a speech by Jagjivan Ram on the question of conversion.
40. *Political Special File No.* 216/1927 (B.S.A.).
41. Ibid.
42. Ibid.
43. Ibid.
44. Ibid.

also by the educated middle class. By putting pressure on conversion these social classes safeguarded their class position i.e. the landlords did reserve labour force to work on lands whether the middle class saw far more political fortune in it. The politically ambitious individuals among Hindus stressed more and more on this issue to reserve vote banks, and on the other hand such individuals among Muslims resented it out of increasing fear psychosis of losing their support in the district board and municipalities elections.[45] The landed classes had their own grievances of securing hired labour because up to this period acute labour problem existed due to the boycott in social services by a community against the other. It needs further discussion. It should be mentioned that this period was marked by the 'period of Sanskritisation.' The lower caste individuals started following the taboos of the upper castes in the false hope of bettering their social status. These social developments might have threatened the interests of the landlords and petty-landlords who drew their sustenance from lands. In this way they utilised the conversion movement launched by the Arya Samaj to safeguard their interests.[46]

Another significant developments of these years was the boycott observed by one community against other. It was also not unprovoked. In October 1925, on the occasions of Muharram and Deshhera festivals, both Muslims and Hindus were encouraged to demonstrate their feelings by boycotting the celebration of the rival community which was previously shared together.[47] The boycott of Chehlum was observed by the Hindus at Bhagalpur, on the other hand Hindus in Sasarma were boycotted by Muslim sweepers in December 1925.[48] Needless to say that these developments resulted in severe threat to the class interests of landlords and bourgeoisie

45. Ibid.
46. Ibid, At several occasions the Hindu Landlord displayed this issue with a view to achieve their objectives.
47. *Administrative Report to the Govt. of Bihar and Orissa* (1924-25), p. 5.
48. Ibid.

etc. It led to propaganda and counter propaganda against Suddhi movement leading to strained relations between Hindus and Muslims.

After discussing the role of different socio-religious organisations, it becomes all the more necessary to underline the part played by different political organisations i.e. the Muslim League, the Hindu Mahasabha, Khaksar and its Hindu counterpart RSS. All these political organisations may be termed basically communal because they promoted obscurantism and religious fundamentalism. Since the top communal leaders were accepted as the spokesman of the Hindus or Muslims, their entire politics and ideology came to be accepted as representing the Hindus or Muslims and their interests and behaviours. This led to the recognition and even direct acceptance to the concept of religious communities in India. It began to be widely assumed that religious communities existed in real life and their interests are dissimilar and divergent.[49]

In this way, they created socio-cultural gap in the social structure and once the gap was created, it kept lingering on and found its manifestation in rural violence on communal line. The partition of Bengal in 1905 was followed by the establishment of Muslim League in 1906 and the Provincial Muslim League saw its birth in March 1908.[50] Sir Ali Imam and Muzherul Haq were elected president and secretary respectively. Both supported nationalism and Hindu-Muslim unity. This was the early years of its inception and the Muslim League and Indian National Congress worked together for a common cause. But after the termination of the Khilafat movement there arose a tremendous split, a gulf which continued ever widening.[51]

After 1930, the influence of the Muslim League began

49. Bipan Chandra, *Nationalism and Colonialism in Modern India*, (Delhi, 1979), p. 257.
50. Ram Sewak, *History of Bihar between two world wars*, (New Delhi, 1985), p. 189.
51. Ibid.

increasing in Bihar and other provinces. Now many nationalist Muslims flirted with the League and from now onwards the way of League's functioning underwent a sea-change.[52] In a meeting of the Provincial Muslim League on 30th June 1933, Mr. Fazlur Rehman, Chairman of the local board addressed his note in Urdu which had obviously communal overtones and did much damage to the existing peace at the mass level between the two communities. He loudly spoke, "since after 1857 the Muhammadans of India are leading a miserable life. They had no influence or respect and only sign of their past glory was the Urdu court language which was also fast disappearing."[53]

It should also be mentioned that the communalists appealed to the past glory and aroused the sentiments of the masses on 'false consciousness' which centred round religion and language. The cry that 'religion in danger' did appeal to the masses due to lack of any political programme on economic lines. In later days, the acceptance of Hindi as a national language was taken to be an attack on the Muslim culture and religion. Such a stereotype was formed among the masses by the communalists. Every action on the national line began to be associated with Hindi, Hinduism and Hindu Raj[54] The Muslims in India were a religious minority. The Muslim masses, middle classes and intellectuals were kept constantly aware of this fact by the imperial writers, administrators, statesmen and active communal leaders both Hindus and Muslims who had their own axes to grind.

Towards the end of October 1933, Mr. Jinnah visited Bihar and his efforts to merge all Muslim parties is one of the significant aspects of political scenario. Mr. Jinnah delivered historical speeches at Patna, Gaya and Biharsharif appealing the Muslim masses to unite.[55]

52. Ibid.
53. *Aryavarta* (Hindi daily, Patna) dated 7th November 1947.
54. Ibid.
55. *Political Special File No.* 169/1933 (B.S.A.).

After the formation of Congress ministry in the province the Muslim League became more active and at several occasions resorted to open violence. Thus, agitational campaigns were launched against the indoctrination of Muslim children in school. Enquiries were set up by the League to expose the communal nature of the Congress administration. All these propaganda led to a situation described below by the collector of Patna district in August 1938.

> "The harping of imaginary grievances and the frequent reiteration of the cry that Muslims are being suppressed by the Congress ministry is making everywhere believe that this is really so."[56]

The tension escalated in several parts of the province after arousal of the people's passion through vicious propaganda. At Teghra in Monghyr district, hand written leaflets purported to have been written on behalf of the Muslim League were found asking people to renounce Hinduism and threatening that there would shortly be no trace of any Hindu temple left in this country.[57]

In May 1939, the serious riot that occurred in Gaya town was the consequence of the arrival of Mr. Jinnah at Gaya one year before. There he made communal slogans and asked the Muslim masses to unite against their enemies.[58] Since then the local leaders of the League have been engaged in an intensive compaign...meetings were organised in mosques where communal hatred was preached.[59] The hoisting of the

56. The Report of the Committee appointed by the Council of All India Muslim League to enquire into Muslim grievances in Congress governed provinces in 1938 (Pirpur Report), in Jamil-ud-din Ahmad (ed), *Historical Documents of the Muslim Freedom Movement*, (Lahore, 1970), pp, 558, 332.
57. *Political Special File No.* 16/1938 (B.S.A).
58. Statement of facts made in the Assembly on behalf of the Govt. by K B. Sahay on 16th May 1939 in *Dr. Rajendra Prasad Correspondence and Select Documents* (edited), Valmiki Chaudhary, Vol. III, p. 340.
59. Ibid.

national flag over the city school in January 1939, and the appearance of the League leaders on the scene led to a serious communal outburst in the town on that day.[60] Immediately before the riot of May came 'Bande Matram' controversy in the Zila school which received support from the Hindu and Muslim guardians. In this period, a series of meetings were addressed by Ghazi Dharampal who under the garb of religion preached the doctrine and programmes of the Muslim League.[61]

In 1940s the activities of the League became more violent. Only in the year 1946 mass scale communal riots did take place and the 'Direct Action Day' call by the League members embittered the feelings at an amazing height. In August 1946 mass murders did take place at Chapra, Islampur, Gaya and several other places following the observance of hartals and bandh. Nehru loudly lamented on the great massacre of Bihar in his private letter to Vallabh Bhai Patel on 5th November 1946 :

> "As a result of Jinnah's call for Direct Action which was publicly celebrated by the Muslim Leage Government of Bengal on 16th August 1946, the riot spread to Hindu majority provinces where the Hindus retaliated against the Muslims."[62]

On the other hand, Hindu communalism was making its progress day by day. The short history of Hindu communal organisations is desirable for having a clear understanding of the role played by them.

The Hindu counterpart of the Provincial League, the Provincial Hindu Sabha met at the first time on 7th July 1919 under the presidency of Maharaja of Darbhanga. In the meeting, much emphasis was laid on the protection of cows.[63]

60. Ibid.
61. Ibid.
62. *The Indian National Movement 1885-1947 : Select Documents*, edited B.N. Pandey, (Delhi, 1979), p. 203.
63. *Political Special File No.* 421/1919 (B.S.A.).

The meeting of All India Hindu Sabha was held in the Congress pandal at Gaya on 30th December 1922 under the presidentship of Madan Mohan Malviya. In this meeting, Malviya insisted more and more on 'Suddhi.'[64] In the course of Suddhi campaigns, forcible conversion was committed resulting in tense social condition. Motilal Nehru on this issue spoke in very strong terms, "The position is getting worse every day...Reports arrive every day of conversion and sometimes the whole villages are converted in a single day."[65]

It is to be noted here that the Suddhi campaign launched by the Hindu communalists had very bad impression on the existing peace at the mass level. In a letter to Dr. Ansari, Hazi Hafiz Hidayat Hussain (one of the founders of All India Muslim League) wrote on the 12th December 1927 :

> "...It is only since 1923 the Suddhi and Sangathan were started that riots began to repeat themselves with frequent obstinacy. The object of the Suddhi was merely political and pursued by physical force, threat, violence and fraud in order to reduce the numerical strength of the Muslims."[66]

In April 1927, Dr. Moonje gave his presidential address to the All-India Hindu Mahasabha preaching the importance of Suddhi and Sangathan.[67] In December 1929, Dr. Moonje and Jagat Narain Lal M.L.C. made several speeches in Bihar on Hindu Sabha and some of their remarks distinctly calculated to attack the Muslim community.[68] As the rift between Muslim League and the Indian National Congress began to grow and the settlement offered by the British Government proved—unsatisfactory, the Hindu Mahasabha

64. *Political Special File No.* 421/1923 (B.S.A.).
65. Motilal Nehru to Jawaharlal Nehru, Sri B.N. Pandey, op. cit., p. 18.
66. Select Correspondence of M.A. Ansari in *Muslims and the Congress* edited by M. Hasan, (Delhi, 1978), p. 41.
67. *Political Special File No.* 16/1928 (B.S.A).
68. *Political Special File No.* 23/1929 (B.S.A.).

gained ground in the political arena. The orthodox Hindus who did not like the liberal attitude of Mahatma Gandhi and the Congress towards the minorities gathered round the banner of Hindu communal groups.

In the month of October 1933 Bhai Paramanand of the Hindu Mahasabha visited Bihar and addressed meetings at Patna and Danapur. He attacked the communal award and blamed the Congress for ruining the prospects of the country. He remarked that 'the British with the assistance of Muslims desired to crush the Hindus, and therefore, Hindus must unite.'[69]

These political developments resulted in intense hostility between the members of the two communities and thus all mutual relations were snapped. In the Seventh Bihar Provincial Conference of the Hindu Mahasabha held at Patna where absence of Hindu militia like Khaksar was largely felt and it was decided to train the Hindus also in the act of valour.[70]

In the succeeding periods, the emergence of the RSS, more militant and fascist organisation of the Hindus worsened the situation all the more. They appealed to the masses on the false hope of bringing good to their community. In this way, they also added some economic programmes like the opening of industrial schools to draw mass support like fascism in Europe. The common masses in the state of utter hopelessness extended their support to the organisation whose very base was 'false and imaginary.' Like European fascism, the RSS leaders often aroused the sentiments of the people along race and culture. It must not be misconstrued as they worked for the welfare of their community but the main objective before them was to capture the seats of M.L.A. and

69. *Political Special File No.* 18/1933 (B.S.A.).
70. *Fortnightly Report to the Govt of Bihar and Orissa* dated 20 April 1940. A circular has been sent by All India Hindu Mahasabha to the provincial branches regarding the formation of Hindu militia i.e. "Ram Sena" and "Bal Sena.".

M.L.C. by organising Hindus.[71]

The rise of RSS struck terror in the hearts of the Muslim masses. From now onwards, even the common muslim people out of fear complex believed in the 'creation of Pakistan.' In this way they helped much to the muslim communalists whose ideal based on the creation of a separate nation for muslims. Reports from several quarters reached to the Government regarding the activities of the RSS volunteers. Ramesh Jha (Minister, Bihar Socialist Party) in a letter to the Premier Bihar wrote, "...The people are feeling quite unsafe and the Government should put an immediate ban on such communal and fascist organisation."[72]

The emergence of communal organisations during these periods was basically centred round the question of share in the loaves of office. From the very beginning the Muslim League was fighting mainly for larger share in the power structure and not on any substantial issue of theological or even broadly of religious nature. The Hindu communalists on the other hand, countered by vehemently opposing demands voiced by the League leadership and putting forward similar demands for the Hindu majority provinces like the Punjab, Bengal and Sindh.[73]

Thus one can see the forces of communal polarisation in these demands and counter demands made by the communalists who were basically interested in the share of spoils rather than building up a just society to fulfil the basic needs of the toiling masses. The elite of the two communities, in order to usurp the emerging opportunities, began to compete with each other in creating support base within their respective

71. *Political Special File No.* 578/1947, p. 8 (B.S.A.). Copy of a Special Branch Officers' Report dated 11.6.47.
72. Ibid., a letter written in Hindi to S.K. Sinha, Premier Bihar by Ramesh Jha (B.S P.) on 22nd Sept. 1947, Letter no. 1879.
73. Mushirul Hasan, "The Delhi Proposals : A Study in Communal Politics," *The Indian Economic and Social History Review*, Vol. VII, pp. 381-85.

community along religious lines. Its emotional potency was their chief asset. In a backward colonial country where emergence of modern capitalism was being throttled in the interests of colonial power, one could hardly expect rational attitudes to strike roots. Also, more the scarcity, greater is the struggle for bringing scarce resources under control whether struggle is waged along class lines or religious lines.

Lastly it is attempted to see the part played by the bureaucracy and the anti-social elements in response to the communal problem. Both these factors are taken together because more often the bureaucracy comes in liaison with the criminal gangs and gonda elements. As it is well known that bureaucracy is a mere shadow of the ruling gamut. Therefore, the bureaucrats design, plan and function what their ruling masters need. If we accuse the ruling party of its basic tendency of 'divide and rule,' how can the bureaucracy be saved from these charges? Sometimes the leading bureaucrats do involve in igniting communal flare up but more often they create a liaison with the hired goondas and gangsters who do the actual fighting.

At Hilsa on 26th June 1893, a communal riot did take place in which the subdivisional officer of Bihar under the instigation of a Muslim subinspector committed violence on Hindus with the help of a 'large body' of the retainers of Muslim landlord.[74] It should be noted that the bureaucracy in league with landlords and the imperialists committed violence.

The landlords and the colonial masters had their own vested interests i.e. of ruling the country with necessary division on caste and communal lines. And the bureaucrats had their own grievances too. Firstly, they had to serve the interests of their masters and secondly to be beneficiaries in loot often happened in communal riots. The Bettiah riot that took place in August 1927 had a similar story where 'loot and

74. Dr. V.C.P. Chaudhary, op. cit., p. 22.

dacoity' was made on behalf of a Hindu subinspector. The riot, though started from the mosque soon spread to Lal Bazar, New market and Purani Gudari areas where only dacoity was made.[75] The incident seemed to be pre planned because discriminate looting was done.[76]

Besides, at several occasions the bureaucrats followed the policy of 'masterly inactivity' and remained silent spectators of the tragic dramas and offered no protection to the people. A riot of such type occurred on 26th October 1946 at the village Inglish Chichraon (Bhagalpur), where arson and looting of Muslim houses continued within half a mile from the police station, but no action was taken to check it.[77]

During October-November riots of 1947, a state of general lawlessness, anarchy and the sense of insecurity prevailed in the whole province. The people had lost faith in bureaucracy because at several places the Government officials were conniving with the rioters in looting instead of giving protection to the people. In the village Badarpur (Nathnagar), a planned attack was made on Hindus by a Muslim mob led by a Muslim constable on 31st October 1946.[78] As the trouble started, some Hindus complained against it in the police station but were refused any help on the plea that 'the area where incident took place is not under their jurisdiction.'[79]

In the situation of lawlessness, confidence ensued among the goonda elements. And the big gangsters, noted criminals and more often the lumpens exploited the situation offered by the Government due to prevailing lawlessness. They started fearlessly displaying caste and creed idioms. They appeared to be the champions of their respective caste and community. When the common people saw no any content of help and

75. *Political Special File No*. 216/1927 (B.S A.).
76. Ibid.
77. *Political Special File No*. 250/1947 (B.S.A.). The Report of the Collector (Bhagalpur) dated 10th Feb. 1947.
78. *Political Special File No*. 250/1947 (B.S.A.).
79. Ibid.

protection in the Government officials, out of fear, they came under the banner of these anti-social elements who offered at least temporary relief to the people. Thus, the socio-political conditions provided opportunities to these elements to display their interests. It helped them to conceal their real character.

During 1946 riots, it is to be noted that those areas remained worse affected by communal violence where big criminal gangs, dacoits and anti-social elements operated. During this period, Patna and Gaya districts were hard hit by communal violence because these areas had previous records of dacoity. In 1930-32, the S.P. (Patna) had shifted his headquarters from Patna to Bihar in order to deal with those gangs.[80] In 1940s, similar dacoity situation had arisen and became a law and order problem.[81]

In the time of communal disturbances these criminal elements whose basic interest was 'to loot and plunder the people' became the master of the situation. Right from Poonpoon (Patna) to Ghosi in Gaya districts, large scale killing was done and worst incendiarism was perpetrated. In most of the cases leadership was provided by the criminal gangs.[82]

An analysis of these riots has shown that the riots erupt spontaneously but are planned in subsequent stages. It is this planned nature of communal riots which is one of the factors influencing the intensity of riots. Further, passivity of the state and popular participation from amongst the lower strata or sections impart ferocity to the riots and accentuate its

80. *Political Special File No.* 314/1947 (B S.A.). The Report given by DIG, CID (Special Branch, Bihar) dated 8th March 1947
81. Ibid.
82 *Political Special File No.* 317/1947 (B S.A.) 'The mob responsible for tragedies in Masaurhi, Poonpoon, Ekengarsarai and Hilsa were led by Mathura Singh of Ghosi Thana and Dhora Singh of Poonpoon who had criminal history.'

A report sent by A.N. Sinha, Special Officer, CID, Bihar, Patna, dated 3.2.1947,

intensity and duration. The normal feature is that incident of communal riots starts with some criminal activity. Further, communalists or instigators who have vested interests, patronise anti-social elements to use them when communal tensions are simmering. It is a fact that spontaneous criminal acts become the immediate cause of communal riots. *It is* not very uncommon that bootleggers and anti-social elements control even the actions of the police. Even anti-social elements and criminals are known to operate on communal and caste divisions at the thana or district level.

To conclude, taking account of the roles played by the social classes *one may remark that behind the trouble lay* the vested interests of the landlords, the Mahajans, doctors and lawyers and the anti-social elements. Mr. Jay Prakash Narayan spoke loudly on the roles played by different classes after 1946 riots in Bihar,

> "...The ignition is supplied by various factors such as communalists, provocateurs, and elements of every type. There are indications that big landlords with vested interests threatened and also the British and communal elements in services fish freely in troubled communal waters."[83]

83. Mr. Jay Prakash Narayan's speech published in *The Star of India*, dated 12th Nov. 1946.

6

Imperial Response to the Problem

"It is interesting to trace British policy since the rising of 1857 and its relation to the communal problem. Fundamentally and inevitably it has been one of preventing the Hindu and Muslim from acting together, and of playing off one community against another . . . ." The fact regarding the policy of the British Government was maintained by Jawahar Lal Nehru in his Autobiography.[1] Nehru was not alone in his assumption but was largely supported by other nationalist thinkers of the time too. Rabindra Nath Tagore tried to point out that much of the Hindu -Muslim bitterness was the creation of British rule in India and was being fostered by the English educated middle class, but the common people were substantially free from such bitterness.[2] In the pre-independence period the theory of communalism most popular with nationalist writers was that communal problem was essentially a product of British policy. Francis Robinson writes,

> ". . . Indian nationalists found the argument particularly attractive and accuse their imperial rulers of having

1. J.L. Nehru, *An Autobiography*, (Oxford, 1982), I I edn., p. 460.
2. S.M. Chand, *National Leaders on Communalism*, (Jaipur, 1985)' pp. 18-19.

broken an evolving synthesis of Hindu-Muslim culture."[3]

But Rabindra Nath Tagore at the same time believed that the British policy of 'divide and rule' could succeed only because something in the internal social, economic and political conditions of society favoured its success. There is a hand of historians who talk of favourable soil. Presiding over the Pabna session of the Provincial political conference in 1907, Tagore declared that the 'alien rulers are trying to excite Hindu-Muslim differences—I am not afraid of that. But we overcome our own divisive tendencies, our own weakness.[4]

In the presence of these contradictory views there is yet another opinion that the charge against the British rulers is overstated. 'The British obviously did not create the Hindu-Muslim communal problem, but they did exploit it for their own purposes from time to time.'[5] Obviously, no one can say that there was not an inherent tendency towards division in India, and with the prospect of the approach of political power, this was likely to grow. It was possible to adopt a policy to tone down this tendency, it was also possible to accentuate it. The Government adopted the latter policy and in every way encouraged fissiparous tendency in the country.[6] To come back to the main point, the British rulers did play an important role in the promotion, spread and growth of communal tension in India. Their role became crucial because they held state power, a crucial determinant in the political fortunes of any ideology or movement.[7] It is also to be noted here that from the very beginning of their rule, the colonial

3. Francis Robinson, *Separatism Among Indian Muslims*. Also see Bipan Chandra, *Communalism in Modern India*, p. 238.
4. Tagore, Presidential address at the Provincial Political Conference, Pabna 1907, Centenary edn. Vol. XII. See S.M. Chand, op. cit., p. 19.
5. K.K. Wadhwa, *Minorities Safeguards in India*, (Delhi, 1975), p. 27.
6 *Jawahar Lal Nehru : Selected Works*, edited by S. Gopal, (New Delhi, 1972), pp. 69-70.
7. Bipan Chandra, op. cit., p. 242.

authorities maintained the policy of divide and rule.[8] Nearly four decades before the outbreak of 1857 revolt a British officer subscribing himself as 'carnaticus' wrote in the 'Asiatic Journal' for May 1821, 'Divide et impera' should be the motto of our Indian administration, whether political, civil or military. Another officer Lt. General John Coke holding the office of commandent at Moradabad wrote.[9]

> "Our endeavour should be to uphold in full force the separatism which exists between the different religious and races." To avoid time and space only a few instances regarding the British policy have been noted.

Following this policy as an essential pre-requisite for Indian administration, the colonial authorities introduced Morley-Minto reforms which largely affected the fabric of communal harmony. Motilal Nehru promptly reacted on this move and he wrote,

> "The great topic of the day is the split caused by Morley between Hindus and Muslims by promising separate representation to the Muslims. The Muhammadans have now begun to abuse the Hindus loudly in their meeting and in the press . . . ."[10]

In the name of providing safeguard to the religious minorities the Government broke the thread of harmony and peace of the two communities and ultimately disrupted their unity against imperial oppression. Consequently communal violence became spasmodic since that period.

Mahatma Gandhi wrote an article in 'Harijan' where he loudly spoke of the real nature of communal violence in India. He remarked,

8. *The Bihar Herald*, July 30, 1927.
9. Ibid.
10. Letter from Motilal Nehru to Jawaharlal Nehru on the rising tension between Hindus and Muslims, dated 1 April 1909 in *The Indian National Movement 1885-1947 : Select Documents* (ed), B.N. Pandey, (Delhi, 1979), p. 18.

"It seems to me that much of this violence is an expression not to much of communal suspicion and hatred, but of the long pent up resentments of the masses against oppression due to the English land holding systems, usurious money lending and heavy taxation . . . The masses always suffer some oppression and, therefore, have resentments which flare up on a shift of control or may be exploited by selfish leaders."[11]

Mahatma Gandhi's statement carries much truth. The strong anti-imperialist resentments accompanied by mass support were often misdirected and termed as the Hindu-Muslim problem. In the October riot of Shahabad (1917), one may notice a strong anti-colonial feeling among the rioters. This fact can be advanced on the basis of the truth that the rioters were seen calling that 'Angrez Ka Raj Uth Gaya' and 'German Ki Jay.'[12] Here it needs some details to clearly see the real facts behind the incident.

In previous years, the question of 'cow sacrifice' had seldom been brought to notice at Shahabad. Never before, it had the history of the resulting breach of peace out of the cow sacrifice.[13] This year it became a vital issue leading to a serious communal trouble.[14] Since the days of Lord Dufferin, the impression in the people's mind has been that Government wants to divide Hindus and Muslims in order to weaken the demand for self-Government. The area that witnessed worse communal antagonisms after the October riots of Shahabad, has largely been under the influence of the Home Rule agitators.[15] They were asking for popular responsibility and

11. *Gandhijee's Selected Letters*, Compiled by Shriman Narain, (Ahmedabad, 1968), pp 332-36.
12. *Political Special File No.* 112/1918 (B.S.A.) Published Oldham's Report on the Bakr-Id trouble of Shahabad in 1917.
13. Ibid.
14. Ibid.
15. *The Behar Herald*, November 10, 1917. Text of Rai Bahadur Purnendu Narain Sinha's speech delivered at Bankipore on 24th October 1917.

popular Government to solve social, economic and political problems. The Home Rule Movement had good impression on people's mind and was welcome to both Hindus and Muslims.[16] This unity resulted in a potent danger to the imperialist forces because they were 'teaching the masses that the British Government is incompetent and so it is collapsing.'[17]

Another interesting side of the picture is that the incident took such a serious dimension due to the negligence and inefficiency on the part of bureaucracy. When Mr. Oldham (Divisional Commissioner) was informed of the trouble, why did not he start for Arrah which is only an hour's journey from Patna instead of waiting there for two days? It is also to note that even after the serious lapses, the officials went unpunished[18] Thus bureaucracy in league with judiciary abetted and perpetuated such crimes and it were the people who suffered. Interestingly enough, Mr. Oldham in his report mentioned that 'The Home Rule agitators were at the bottom of the trouble partly to discredit the leaders and partly to criss-cross and confuse the mass movement.'[19] Therefore it is very hard to negate imperial high handedness behind the whole plot of massacre.

In 1915, the incident of the same nature had taken place in Kanchanpur (Fatwah) where no less than 50,000 persons collected from the different areas and it was characterised as a 'rebellion' by Mr. Godbole, the then SDO at Barh.[20] But soon it was magnified into Hindu-Muslim problem.

The Chittagong (Bengal) riot of August 1931 had the same characteristic. It did not have a background of Hindu-

16. *The Behar Herald*, November 10, 1917.
17. *Political Special File No.* 112 1918 (B.S,A.). See Oldham's Report (published), p. 24.
18. *Amrita Bazar Patrika*, 8 April, '1918. The news captioned 'Official Genesis of Arrah Riots" published.
19. *Political Special File No.* 112/1918, p. 24 (B S.A).
20. *Amrita Bazar Patrika*, 8th April 1918. At a meeting of the Supreme Council on the 22nd March 1918, answer given by Sri William Vincent to Mr. Abdul Rahim's question.

Muslim tension. But ever since the Chittagong Armoury Raids of April 1930 by the terrorists, acute tension persisted between Europeans and middle class Hindus of the town. On 30 August, a senior police official called a Muslim meeting on the premises of the police station and openly incited the audience to attack Hindus.[21] All political suspects were rounded up in a midnight raid and tortured under the direction of the European A.S.P. in the presence of several other Europeans . . . . Several raids into nearby villages were later organised under the European officers.[22]

Bureaucracy was the most potent and faithful tool of imperial administration in India to safeguard their vested interests. The bureaucrats were the sole arbitor of the Governmental policies on whom vested the responsibilities of executing their policies once planned by the ruling masters. There are several instances of official negligence on the part of communal problem. Besides, several instances can be cited of the bureaucracy following the policy of 'masterly inactivity.' The riot that originated and immediately assumed wider dimensions in Shahabad in 1917 is one of the examples of official negligence, complete liaison between bureaucracy and judiciary and of the part played by the police in bringing the actual trouble. The subinspector of Shahabad in a confidential letter to the Commissioner writes, "he had been thinking for the disunion for the last 25 years, he further says, he should have taken the Shahabad matter into his hands to reconcile both parties but it is his principle not to leave a thing unfinished . . . ."[23] What was his principle?

The part played by the officials in disturbing the existing peace and harmony could not remain unexposed for a

21. Tanik Sarkar's article 'Communal Riots in Bengal' in M. Hasan, *Communal and Pan-Islamic Trends in Colonial India* (ed), (Delhi, 1981), p. 304.
22. Ibid.
23. Tirhut Commissioner's File No. 97-C/1917 (B.S.A.) quoted in B.B. Mishra's *Mahatma Gandhi's Movement in Champaran*) (ed, (Patna, 1963), p. 416.

long time. The nationalist leader and their chief spokesman tried continuously to unravel the mask and condemned their policies of 'benevolent neutrality.' Abdul Ghani, a non-cooperator of Shahabad, contributes an article to the 'Tarun Bharat' (Patna) in the course of which he refers to the unsettled condition of the country attributing it to the diplomacy of bureaucracy and makes the following statements with reference to the coming Bakr-Id :

> "Various rumours are being spread on behalf of the bureaucracy. Let it remember that its tricks have already become public. I would frankly ask my Muslim brethren—Are the Hindus more bitter enemies of Islam than the Englishmen? I would ask my Hindu brethren to avoid falling into the trap of bureaucracy. The bureaucracy wants that the two communities should fight against each other. We pray to God that unity between the Hindus and the Muslims be strengthened in this country so that the policy of bureaucracy may be defeated and the western rulers may leave India."[24]

One may remark here that the bureaucracy was shamelessly involved in their nefarious activities of disrupting the evolving synthesis between the masses of the two communities. One may also locate a direct connection between the masters and their ruling servants who tirelessly followed the masterly policy of 'divide and rule.' Not only this, some nationalist newspapers and the periodicals involved in accusing this policy of the Government and in condemning the activities of the bureaucrats were kept in constant watch and sometimes penalised for this offence. The literature having contents of 'Hindu-Muslim Unity' and anti-imperialist discussion was immediately proscribed by the Government. The "Tarun Bharat" for publishing materials to this nature was proscribed and cases were lodged against its editors.[25] A

24. *Tarun Bharat* (Patna), 22 July 1923.
25. *Political Special File No.* 172/.923 (B.S.A.). Confidential letter no 5222, from the D.I.G., C.I.D. to the Chief Secretary, Govt. of

poem was published on 9 September 1923 in which the bureaucracy was charged with all the ill-will existing at the mass level in both the communities. The content of the poem runs as follows :

Ever since its advent
The bureaucracy has been playing at a game.
Having made India dependent
it has been enjoying external happiness.
It has been behaving wickedly !
Strange is its policy
Externally does it look white,
but internally it is black.
Alas ! this bureaucracy
has ruined India."

At another place the District Magistrate has been termed as 'the white elephant' and their actions as the Chairman of the District Boards have been characterised as 'harmful to the Indians as those of step-mothers are to their step-sons.'[26]

It is to be noted that the colonial regime had by the 1920s evolved an extensive system of police-reporting, intelligence-gathering and Press Censorship and other laws to control the press. But this machinery of suppression was directed against and used almost wholly against the nationalist movement. Even the slightest effort to produce 'disaffection' and 'sedition' was taken note of and often acted against.[27] In this the government was rigid, active, vigilant and effective. On the other hand, the Government of India refused to take action against propagation of virulent communal ideas and

Bihar and Orissa. .... 'A full translation of the letter headed "Text for Hindus and Muslims of Bihar," published at p. 2 in 'Tarun Bharat'. . . . is exceedingly mischievous and objectionable under section 124-A and 153-A, I.P.C.'

26. *The Tarun Bharat*, April 23, 1923.
27. *Political Special File No.* 173/1923 (B.S.A.).

communal hatred. The rare action was taken only in the worst cases of religious attacks when religious susceptibilities were hurt so as to avoid extreme excitement which might threaten law and order.[28] But the same legislative, police and administrative machinery suffered from fits of absent mindedness and relative inactivity where even the most vicious forms of communal propaganda and other activities giving direct incitement to communal murder and rioting and in general perpetuation of communalism were concerned. Numerous instances of this double standard can be given. For example, while discussing the communal riots of Bengal in 1907, Sumit Sarkar has pointed out:

> "Ibrahim Khan, the author of that communal 'Red Pamphlet' was let off with a warning, while Liakat Hussain and Abdul Gafur were being hounded down for sedition."[29]

The communal and British-supported newspapers were given free reign to publish and highlight sensational reports of alleged communal occurrences, including rape, abduction and killing, in terms which were blatantly designed to incite extreme communal emotion among the readers. The 'Aryavarta' (Hindi) and the 'Indian Nation' (English) both published from Patna had strong anti-Muslim bias, but was characterised as the 'nationalist' newspaper by the Government officials.[30] The Muslim communal newspaper i.e. "Sada-i-Aam" too was patted and encouraged by the ruling party. They seldom became the victim of Governmental wrath.[31]

The British rulers followed the policy of 'religious neutrality' and transcended communal bias at least in theory but in practice they seldom conformed to this principle. They

28. Bipan Chandra, op. cit., p. 280.
29. Sumit Sarkar, *The Swadeshi Movement in Bengal 1903-1908*, New Delhi (1973), p. 80.
30. *The Fortnightly Press Report*, dated 3 June 1941, p. 3.
31. *The Behar Herald*, dated 16th November 1946,

ruled the country with 'divine dispensation' and their claim of being secular in Indian administration was negated at several places, particularly at the time when and where the nationalist forces were at work. The movement of the people on the part of national independence seemed alien to the colonial rulers who followed the masterly policy of 'divide and rule,' 'concession and repression' and at times patting and conniving one community against another, one caste against another to give further sustenance to their rule. This policy was followed and maintained throughout the whole period of their colonial rule. To what extent our 'white rulers' were secular in Indian matters can be judged by the initiatives taken by them in cow-protection agitation once led by the native vested interest groups. In London, after the announcement of Morley-Minto reforms, several associations for the protection of Indian cattle were formed. The 'British Association for the protection of Indian cattle' counted for its supporters on the 'members of Parliament and many other influential persons.'[32] In a letter written by Mr. H.B. Holme on behalf of Indian people he made an appeal to all Indians i.e. "Maharajas, Rajas, Landholders, Jagirdars, cow-protectors, cow worshippers, secretaries of Samajes and Sabhas, spiritual leaders of different Hindu communities to wake up and awaken the sleeping,"[33] He further remarks that 'this is the right time for the test of your patriotism.'

To provide justification to this clarion call on the part of Hinduism, the imperial rulers appalled to the past and loudly spoke that 'your ancesters have worshipped the cow, the great law giver Manu has laid it down that the cow should be honoured.' Are you not the descendants of the same Hindu ancestors?[34] In this way they aroused the feelings

32. *Bihar and Orissa Police Abstract of Intelligence, 1912*, p. 5. A letter from H.B. Holme Esq, I.C.S. Under secretary to the Govt. of India, Depatt. of Revenue and Agriculture to K.S. Jassawala, President founder of the 'British Association for Protection of Indian Cattle,' Letter No. 96L 1693 dated 6th May 1910.

33. *Bihar and Orissa Police Abstract of Intelligence* 1912, p. 5.

34. Ibid.

of the Hindu population and brought considerable damage to the existing harmonious life of the two communities. All such socio-religious organisations which were previously active in this agitation were let loose. The confidence ensued among the members of these organisations due to the official support for this cause. The situation became very tense and several cases of forcible ban on the cow slaughter by the Hindus have come into existence. A serious trouble was reported from the village Sabalbigha (Monghyr) in June 1912.[35] A large crowd of Hindus assembled in the said village and tried their best to stop sacrifice. In spite of the presence of the authorities they assaulted the Musalmans, looted their houses and abused them.[36]

It must not be misunderstood that the British administrators were favouring Hindus and their religion and they were the saviour of the protection of cattle. If the cow was very sacred to Hindus, they regarded it as the 'mother' but not for the white people whose favourite dish was beef. Neither they were champions of Hinduism because they ever boasted that Christianity was superior to all nor the cows were sacred to them. The main intention behind the initiatives taken by them in cow protection was partly to create reaction among the people and partly to win the heart of the Hindu masses. Far from it, the real objective was to confuse and criss-cross the national movement. The Hindu people were made to believe that their patriotism lies in the observance of the past glory and adherence to their religious belief.

These political developments largely antagonised the Muslim population who once believed to fight unitedly against the foreign imperialism.[37] Now they started thinking of their Hindu brethren 'as enemy out of reaction' and solely relied on the 'sympathy and help by the Government.'[38] The low

35. Ibid. Supplement to Bihar Abstract No. 10, p. 67. dated 8th June 1912.
36. *Bihar and Orissa Police Abstract of Intelligence* 1912, p. 5.
37. Ibid., Bengal Abstract, dated 27.4.1912, para. 1455, p. 26.
38. Ibid

level official workers stoop to the formation of propaganda and largely poisoned the ears of the members of one community against the other.[39] It is interesting in this connection to note that no any legal action was taken. In this way, both the Hindus and the Muslims *fighting together* helped the colonial rulers in their objectives of keeping the national tide at its low ebb. It must not be misconstrued that the Britishers were pro-Hindu or pro-*Muslim. They* supported either Hindu or Muslim communalism to blunt the edge of nationalism.[40]

In spite of all these, the objective behind the rule of India did not remain uexposed for a long time. There were numerous educated Indians *who believed that* 'India was not governed for the good of the Indians, but was to serve, feed and fatten the English.'[41] It has been further remarked that,

> "The bureaucratic Feringees (foreigners) tried their utmost to put down the nationalist Movement in India with iron hand. . . . They are *adopting their old policy* of 'Divide and Conquer' once followed at the time of great revolt of 1857."

The official patronage to anti-cow slaughter agitation and incompetency of the Government officials in having control over the resulting disturbances,[42] *alienated the* Muslim masses and therefore, they became critical to the imperial rulers. Several right thinking Muslims criticised the Govern-

39. Ibid., para, 806, p. 294. The S.I. of Bihar P.S. produced a patia in Hindi which was to the effect that Hindus should not sell cattle to Muhammadans. *The circulation* of the patias has originally been started by Excise head peon.
40. Bipan Chandra, op. cit., p.
41. Bihar and Orissa Police Abstract of Intelligence 1913, para-861 p. 312. Text of a proscribed leaflet 'Liberty' (Ambala), 20 July 1913.
42. Ibid., para. 7-8, p. 23 dated 25.4.1942. At several places 'Gowshalas' for the *protection of* cattle have been opened. Mr. Lewis, the Manager of the Bettiah Raj became the president and the famous "Lewis Gowshala" at Bettia his named after him.

ment's actions and attitudes towards the Muhammadan community and appealed to the masses to join the Hindus in politics. They largely felt that there would be 'no concession without agitation.'[43]

The talk of Hindu-Muslim unity among the Muslims on one hand and the natural affiliation of the Muslim educated persons to the Balkan affairs in which England was badly engaged, apprehended and threatened the interests of the colonial regime. The favour of Indian Muslims did fell on the Turkish side, and every step of the British power in Balkan was condemned and challenged by the Muslims in India. To divert the attention of the people from the Balkan affairs, the Government raised mosque controversy by demolishing a part of the mosque in Cawnpore to make roadways[44] (Emphasis mine). Once the issue was raised, the feelings of the Muslim students in particular and the lower class people in general were excited in Patna.[45]

At Deoghar. Biharsharif, Muzaffarpur, Monghyr and Ranchi the frenzy of excitement was largely felt consequent to the Kanpur mosque affair. At Deoghar, both the Hindu and the Muslim communities agreed in condemning the action of the Government in the matter. Meetings were held at several places in the province in this connection. In a meeting at Bankipore on the 31st August 1913, Mr. Mazharul Haq a prominent and respected Musalman expressed his deep concern and said that 'the Government had no right to interfere in their religion.'[46]

Having raised this issue. the Government cautiously watched the activities of the people. The news that the issue of the Balkan war has been relegated to the background and the chief subject of discussion among the people about Cawnpore

43. Ibid., Bengal Abstract, dated 27.4.1912, para. 1453, p. p. 26.
44. Ibid., para. 1012, p. 356, Patna, dated 9.8.1913.
45. Ibid., para. 902, Patna, dated 16.9.1913.
46. Ibid., *Bihar Abstract*, 30.8.1913, para. 938, p. 333.

Mosque riot consoled the alien rulers (Emphasis mine).[47] The issue had deliberately been created and it was 'merely an incidental expression of resentment' and 'was generated by another cause.'[48]

The British Indian administrators did not support a particular 'community' or communalism for the love of that 'community' or communalism. The aim of the British policy was to check the politicisation of the Indian people, to curb their consolidation and unification and to disrupt the process of the Indian nation-in-tne-making.[49] Once the anti-imperia-nationalist movement arose, the policy was also directed towards checking its growth, dividing-its actual or potentialist supporters and preventing Muslims from joining it. To meet the nationalist onslaught and to perpetuate their own rule, the British needed to find support among some sections of the Indian people, to create some political support base. The long term policy adopted was that of stimulating communal antagonism and communal politics and organisations through appropriate short-term administrative policies which could have a certain diversity to suit the given movement as well as the potentialities and the outlook of the given administrators.[50] It would divide the Indians, make their fight each other as enemies and secure the active or passive support of communal forces for colonial rule because they would treat the other community as the main and immediate enemy.

One reason that enabled the colonial state to support communalism and to make this policy a success was the common social base of both in the jagirdari elements in general and the landlords and the bureaucrats in particular who felt threatened along with the colonial state by the radical changes in thc political and economic structure

47. Ibid., *Ranchi Abstract*, dated 23.8.1913, para 956. p. 341. "It has been reported that the Muslims of the town are little intersted in the Balkan war The chief subject of conversation is the Cawnpore mosque affair."
48. Ibid., *Hazaribagh Abstract*, 19.8.1913, para. 959, p. 341.
49. Bipan Chandra, op. cit., p. 246.
50. Ibid.

projected by the anti-imperialist forces.[51]

The policy of divide and rule was complex and subtle. Both its critics and those who criticise them have tended to a rather simplistic or crude understanding of it. It seldom, except perhaps near the end, took the form of a conspiracy by the officials. As we see that the communalists were seldom given open and all out support by the colonial state. They were encouraged through the ready acceptance of their demands and non-action against their ideological misdemeanours and extension of official patronage and so on. The "Behar Herald" on the 4th November 1922 comments in its editorial note that "the Britishers in India has, as a rule, been exploiting to his advantage the racial differences of the indigenous population....It has been described by a famous writer as the fundamental condition of foreign supremacy in India." It has been further remarked that "a casual reading of the speeches and writings of responsible British officials and public men will show the truth of this observation."[52]

It has been discussed above that the British officials seldom encouraged the divisive forces directly. But through their actions, as the part of their colonial administration they indirectly supported these divisions and played one caste, group and community against the other. The communal tension at Phulwari (Patna) in the month of July was consequent to the deliberate Government's policy of playing one community against the other. The issue was raised on the pretext of the Muhammadans' opposition to the music before mosque.[53] As the tension apprehended, the local members of both the communities called a meeting[54] in which it was remarked that "in 1893 there was a civil suit by the Hindus

51. Ramvilas Sharma, *Bharat Mein Angrezi Raj aur Marxvad* (Hindi), Delhi (1982), Vol. I, p. 441.
52. *The Behar Herald*, 4th November, 1942. Editorial note captioned 'Feeding the Flame'.
53. *The Behar Herald*, July 24, 1926.
54. Ibid. The meeting was attended by Dr. Rajendra Prasad and Maulvi S.M. Hafiz, Secretary 'Anjuman Mahafizat.'

for the declaration of their rights to take a procession with music on the road, which was opposed by the Muslims.... The suit was compromised.... But this year for reasons best known to the Government, the Government granted a license to carry a procession with music in spite of the opposition by the Muslims." In post-indendence India too, one can notice the developments taking place in different parts of the country following the controversy raised by the Government after opening the 'Ram Janam bhoomi" lock on the one side and the popular case of a Muslim woman on the other hand.[55]

Far from it, at several occasions the police men were directly engaged in inciting the members of one community against the other. There were strong rumours in the public that the CID people make every effort 'to excite people and create communal feeling.' A story of this peculiar nature can be cited from happening in Patna City that took place in April 1931. The story follows as:

'Two men, one posing as a Hindu and the other as a Muhammadan were washing hands after having eaten something, when a drop of water happened to touch the body of the Hindu, who became enraged and violently rebuked the so-called Muhammadan for his carelessness. The Muhammadan in the meanwhile tried to run away, but his turban accidently fell, and on his head was discovered a tuft of hair (tiki), which led people to believe thatthe man was a Hindu in disguise.![56] The general impression was that both the men were CID people, and were trying to create communal feeling among the people.[57] It may be remarked here that the Government was instrumental in bringing about communal fracas, as it has previously been done at Kanpore. These activities were solely directed towards checking the masses

55. *The Times of India*, dated 22nd February 1986. It led to disturbances at several places in the country i.e. Anantnag, Nawadah, Uttar Pradesh etc.
56. *Political Special File No.* 151/1931, p. 4 (B.S.A.). Extract from a special Branch Inspector's Report, dated Patna, 13th April 1931.
57. Ibid.

from taking part in non-cooperation and Civil Disobedience movements launched by the Congress. Not only this, when the trouble did arise in a certain part of the province due to the officials mediocrity, the Government took every pain to term it 'as the trouble out of the Congress activities.'[58]

In this atmosphere of lawlessness, the general people lost their faith in Government machinery and the bureaucracy thoroughly became unpopular. In most of the cases, crime committed by these elements were whitewashed by the colonial authorities and they were seldom punished for their fault. A similar event did take place in Sasaram in 1925 when 'stoppage of a religious procession without any reasonable ground' by the then subdivisional officer of Sasaram largely antagonised the Hindu population.[59] The said SDO was a Muhammadan. The incident resulted in acute tension between the masses of the two communities.

In order to combat the real danger, the local Hindus and Muhammadans of Sasaram held a public meeting on the 19th February 1925. Mr. Abdul Wahab acted as the president and the resolutions were made appealing the Government that 'severe actions should be taken against the ill manner and bad conduct of the officer' who making alliance with some influential persons of the town aroused the sentiments of the Hindu masses.[60] In the same resolution the subdivisional officer has been characterised as a 'hungry lion.' It is quite interesting to note here that inspite of a large protest made by the people, the SDO went scot free and his actions were justified by the Government.[61]

The British also encouraged communalism through non-action against it. Certain positive measures which the state

58. *Administrative Report to the Govt. of Bihar and Orissa.*
59. *Political Special File No.* 51/1925, p. 2 (B.S.A.). "Protest against the action of the 'SDO Sasaram in prohibiting Hindu procession on the occasion of 'Basant Panchmi' ceremony."
60. Ibid., Resolutions made in a public meeting on 19.2.1925, Abdul Wahab acted as its president.
61. Ibid. Letter from Chief Secretary, Govt. of Bihar and Orissa dated 17.3.1925, p. 3.

alone could undertake were needed to check the growth of communal violence. The British failure to undertake them seemed as an indirect encouragement to communal forces.

First of all the Government of India refused to take action against propagation of virulent communal ideas and communal hatred. The communalists used almost every form of vicious and inflammatory propaganda: speeches, rumours, popular press, leaflets, pamphlets, poems. dramas, novels, satire, caricature, parody. Rarely did the Government take any action to curb it or punish its perpetrators. A Hindi booklet entitled "Hindu Samaj Chetawani No. 1" was proscribed by the Government on the plea that 'the booklet contained exciting songs liable to promote communal passion.'[62] But it is very interesting and rather remarkable to note that no any legal action was taken against its publisher and writer.[63]

One may quote numerous instances of this type regarding the policy of the Government. But, on the other hand, those newspapers were kept in constant vigilance which were critical to the government and often dared publishing the real account of the happenings. The national daily '*Dawn*' was warned at several times because it made the activities of the Government public. Several newspapers in Hindi and English published inflammatory accounts but went unnoticed and the Urdu daily 'Sada-e-Aam' when complained against it, received warning for this from the Government.[64] For blaming the Government in the public and for making their policies exposed to everyone, Sada-e-Aam was proscribed and its editor

62. *Political Special File No.* 209/1947 (B.S.A.). A Hindi booklet 'Hindu Samaj Chetawani no. 1' has been proscribed. The booklet was written by Pandit Sukhdeo Sharma 'Karmkandi,' Silaut (Muzaffarpur). It was published from 'Chand Press' ('ehanabad) by Pandit Chandradeo Sharma, reports CID Bihar, special Branch dated 7th May 1947.
63. Ibid.
64. *The Behar Herald*, dated 9 November 1946.

Mr. S. Nazir Haidar was acquitted.[65]

It should be also discussed in brief that the literature having anti-British contents was immediately proscribed by the officials in the name of maintaining communal harmony. Such a literature was branded and grouped 'communal literature' only to provide justification to their actions. "AAPAS KA TAKRAR", a Hindi booklet was proscribed under the Press Act 1931 on the charge of spreading communal hatred in the province. But mainly the booklet preached Hindu-Muslim harmony and asked the people to join hands against the common enemy i.e. the foreign imperialism.[66] In the booklet it was stated that,

> "...the Hindus and Muslims both are the sons of the same 'mother' India.... By fighting together both of you will be weakened and the reign of the Britishers will prolong."

The British administration also practised a policy of relative inactivity and irresponsibility in dealing with communal riots. When the riots occurred, they were not crushed energetically. The well-known steel-frame strangely became inefficient and the trigger-happy policy developed qualms of conscience in using counter-violence. The administration also seldom made proper preparations or adopted preventive measures to meet situations of communal tension. This dereliction of elementary administrative duty was particularly glaring because most of these situations, such as coincidence of Holi and Muharram, cow-slaughter or protest against public sale of beef, could be forseen months ahead of time. Even otherwise a communal riot seldom occurred without warning signals days and weeks ahead. For a riot to occur, tension had to build up to the requisite pitch. This took some time. The C.I.D. and the intelligence system functioned

65. *The Searchlight*, dated 23rd December 1947.
66. *Political Special File No.* 247/1947 (B.S.A.). A Hindi booklet 'AAPAS KA TAKRAR' was published from Kala Mandir Press, Sitamarhi.

fairly well. Provocations such as music before mosque, organisation of sacrificial cow processions and the efforts to stop them were normally known to the police and magistracy. The administration invariably got enough time to take precautionary measures. That administrative inactivity in the face of communal tension was not the result of an inherent difficulty in dealing with it is shown by the fact that whenever the administration decided to prevent a riot or to suppress it, the task was performed efficiently.[67]

A large number of contemporary public persons and the press expressed the opinion that the British authorities deliberately instigated and engineered or at least connived at communal riots, especially when faced with nationalist or class upsurge, through agent provocateurs, aid to the instigators and organizers of the riots and such other methods. Recent historical researches at the micro-level tend to confirm this view.[68]

Extreme communal feelings or involvement of religion in politics could also lead to mass politics and to popular outbreaks which could turn against the colonial authorities and simultaneously with communal or religious feelings, promoted anti-imperialism.[69] In this way, sometimes communalism was clearly undesirable to the Government of its edge turned against the Government. We may, for example, notice the fate of the militant Khaksar Movement 1930s. This movement was based on artisans and lower class Muslims and previously backed by the landlords.[70]

The Khaksar party was not merely communal but was

67. G.R. Thursby, *Hindu-Muslim Relations in British India*, (Leiden, 1975), pp. 83, 88. Also see, Tanik Sarkar, "Communal riots in Bengal," p. 290.
68. Sumit Sarkar, op. cit , pp. 451-52.
Also see Tanik Sarkar, op. cit., p. 91.
Also see Bipan Chandra, op. cit., p. 285.
69. *Political Special File No.* 247/1947 (B.S.A.).
70. *Fortnightly Report to the Govt. of Bihar and Orissa*, dated 3rd Feb. 1940.

also developing as a mass movement and posing a threat to law and order.[71] It was anti-Congress and at the same time becoming anti-Government.[72] The more *middle class based,* elitist and politically passive Rashtriya Swayam Sevak Sangh was carefully watched for any anti-Government potentialities, but was left alone for the time being when it was found that it had no immediate intention of opposing the Government.[73]

This fear of communalism becoming a popular force which migh turn against the Government also explains certain other aspects of Government policy. Thus, the British officials were highly critical of the Arya Samaj because, though it tended to foster *communal politics* and *increased* communal violence, it was suspected of also being anti-British.[74] The move of the Khaksar party though basically,.a communal organisation, became a potent danger to the Government. Like other communal organisations, its leaders also pursued the tactics of pressurising the central and provincial Government 'to concede to the pocket demands of the Muslims of Bihar.'[75] On the other hand their activities were solely directed against the British when Allama Masherequi loudly declared that "the policy of the Britishers created disunity between Hindus and *Muslims*···." He further says, "the Britishers are seasoned politicians and their intentions and; 'Quit India declaration' are but great political bluff.... The administration of India has deliberately been made insufficient due to the Britishers intrigue.[76] The anti-British approach of the Khaksars was quite unwelcome to the British administrators. They charged this organisation of being a 'foreign element' and backed by foreign hands to

71. *Political Special File No.* 400/1947 (B.S.A).
72. Ibid.
73. Ibid.
74. Bipan Chandra, op. cit., p. 249.
75. *Political Special File No.* 400/1947 (B.S.A.). The Report of the DIG, CID Patna, dated 19.4.1947.
76. *Political Special File No.* 400/1947 (B.S.A.). Published text of Allama Masherequi's speech delivered at Gandhi Maidan Patna on 19.4.47.

disrupt colonial administration.[77] It is very common to accuse the neighbour rather than to keep his house in order. It is also practised in present day India. Behind every disturbance, it is quite fashionable to seek foreign hands to cover up internal politico-economic disorder.

The policy of inactivity was to cost thousands of lives during the communal killings of 1946-47. Both in Bengal and Bihar, officials from the highest to the lowest ranks remained passive, inactive, indifferent, irresolute and supine in the face of massive killings, butchery and one sided programmes, when elementary administrative integrity and activity could have saved thousands of lives. During this period, 'all communal bodies proliferated, and communal elements were let loose which resulted in genocide.[78] Really it was a blot on the part of the British Government that ever boasted of civilized and cultured heritage. Bewildered Churchill expressed deepest sense of horror at the wholesale massacre of the people in Bihar on the 12th December 1946 in the House of Commons, London. Mr. Churchill remarked,

> "Bihar has put into the shade the Armenian atrocities with which Gladstone at once stirred the moral sense of liberal Britain."[79]

Thus, the administration's inactivity during communal riots had very drastic consequences. Once people could not get police protection during communal riots, they were forced to organise self-defence along caste or communal lines and to rely upon their respective communal organisations. One thing must be mentioned here that in the last phase of their rule, the colonial administrators openly incited communal violence to discredit the Congress Government already functioning in several provinces. By letting loose all communal elements

77. Ibid. The report of the D I.O. Patna on 19.4.47.
78. *The Bihar State Killing* 1946 (Published). The official statement and Resolution of Bihar Provincial Muslim League on the Bihar massacre, p. 1.
79. Ibid.

even at the last hour, the imperial policy worked to make the people believe that Indians were not equipped to 'self-rule.'

To sum up, it needs mention here that what were involved in this policy were state power and the state always has immense power for good or evil. This is even more true of the colonial state which covered wider areas of life, had greater administrative constitutional power. It alone could take action against malicious and provocative communal propaganda, vicious lies and rumour-mongering. It alone could take preventive police measures in case of communal tension. It alone had the legal sanction and the requisite apparatus for using force against rioters, it alone could punish the instigators or organizers of riots.

Conclusion

In conclusion, it must be pointed out that communal problem is very basic to the colonial administration in this country. The underdeveloped colonial economy frustrated all the hopes of better prospect of the toiling masses who were crying under Zamindari oppression. The moneylenders proved far more oppressive to them. These economic tendencies generated a sense of insecurity among the people and this sense of deprivation and social frustration found its expression in many perverse form, communal violence being one of them. The masses under relative backwardness failed to realize the real issues. In this way, the real issue remained obscure and the very false and imaginary one predominated.

Secondly, the want of clear ideals and objectives in our struggle for freedom undoubtedly helped the spread of communalism. The masses saw no clear connection between their day to day sufferings and the fight for swaraj. They fought well enough at times by instincts but that was feeble weapon as Nehru wrote, which could be easily blunted or even turned aside for other purposes. There was no reason behind it, and in periods of reaction it was not difficult for the communalists to play upon this feeling and exploit it in the name of religion. It is nevertheless, extraordinary how the bourgeois, both among the Hindus and the Muslims, succeed in the sacred name of religion, in getting a mass sympathy and support for programmes and demands which had absolutely nothing to do with the masses or even the lower middle class.

Everyone of the communal demands put forward by any communal group is, in the final analysis, a demand for jobs, and these jobs could go to a handful of the upper middle class. There is, of course, the demand for special and additional seats in the legislatures, as symbolising political powers, but this too is looked upon chiefly as the power to exercise patronage. Their narrow political demands, benefiting at most a small number of the upper middle classes, and often creating barriers in the way of national unity and progress were cleverly made to appear the demands of the masses of that particular religious group.

In this way, the political reactionaries came back to the political field in the guise of communal leaders, and the real explanation of the various steps they took was not so much their communal bias as their desire to obstruct political advance. And thus behind the facade of religion, vested interests particularly the Zamindars and the capitalists were fighting against the interests of the poor masses. It has been discussed previously that the communal organisations were primarily backed by the Hindu and the Muslim landlord who used it as an instrument to keep the oppressed people disunited and politically vulnerable. Later on, these techniques were seized on by the Marwaris who were engaged mainly in trading activities. At several places it had been complained by the people that 'the Hindus and the Muslims of a particular area liked to live amicably but the situation of frenzy, loot and arson was almost created by the Marwaris.'[1] It may significantly be posed, how communal violence did benefit these trading communities or what interests did it serve them?

It is also to be pointed out that as the danger of Bengal partition on communal lines became a grim living reality, the dominant section of the Hindu nationalist leadership started becoming angry so much against the British, as against the Muslims also. This naturally made the communal situation far worse, tended to drive a deeper wedge between Hindus and

1. See Appendix-IV.

Muslims and only brought grist to the mill of the British imperialist. What was the reason behind the hostility towards the Muslim after the partition of Bengal? Its answer should be sought in the policy of the colonial ruler and the political developments of the period.

It is maintained by the historians and other social scientists as well that communal riots is consequent to communal politics. In short, communalism is prior to communal violence. But one may argue that communalism developed when the communication link between the people living in different parts of the country became easier. It is because, the communalists appealed to the religious belief of the people and it is all India in nature. But communal riots have some local characteristics. Most of the riots that took place before 1930s (when communalism and communal riots were not mixed), tended to operate in a particular area or province. It could be easily localised. But as soon as communal politics tended to promote communal violence, the riots had wide repercussions. The atrocities committed on the members of a particular community in a particular region or states was resented by the people in other provinces. In this way, rumours were set in motion by the press, platform and such other agencies for the growth of communalism.

APPENDICES

APPENDIX-I

Extract from the Dawn dated 5.5.47

"Technique of Riots in Bihar Districts : Planned Attacks : *Police Support*"

The conduct of the police all through the carnage was most reprehensible. Evidences collected by the League show that, 'with a few noble exceptions, the members of the Bihar Police, both armed and civil, were working in complete collaboration with the riots'. At many places they remained silent spectators of the tragic dramas and offered no protection to the victims. In many places they seized lawfully held arms on the assurance to protect and then quickly withdrew from the scene leaving them to be slaughtered . . . . At some places the S.I. of police even lent their own guns of the police station and the Government Armouries to the attacking mobs.

The Bihar Premier Mr. Sri Krishna Sinha's relatives tried to interfere in the course of the judicial and executive functions of the District Magistrate, Monghyr. He arrived at Monghyr on the 27th act. 1964... . On 28th Oct. he shifted to the house of D.M. Mr. Omar . . . . On the 28th the riots started in Monghyr . . . . and *continued till 9th Nov.* . . . the intruder had taken charge not only of the telephone but was present at the D.M's table and he was actually working as the D.M. all but in name.

On the 28th Oct. 1946 S.M. Yasin, the gun maker apprehended communal troubles at Monghyr and approached

Mr. Rajeshwari Prasad, the S.P. at Monghyr and requested him to protect, but the later refused to provide guards and directed him to deposit the entire arms and ammunitions to the Government.

When all the Hindu as well as Muslim shops of arms and ammunitions were closed by the Govt. another relative of Mr. Sinha approached the D.M. for licence . . . the D.M. ordered his licence clerk to issue a licence which was handed over to the Premier's nephew without any enquiry into the character of the applicant which is the general rule.

While all the shops were closed under the order of the Govt. authority, still another relative of the Premier of Bihar approached the D.M. and in the name of the repairing of his gun, one or two Hindu shopkeepers were allowed to open their shops . . . . All this happened during the massacers while rioting was still going on.

APPENDIX-II

"Majority Community Guilty of Heinous Crimes."
"Have Committed Act of Abject Cowardice and Barbarity."
"Terrible and Gruesome Things Happened in Bihar."

—Jaiprakash Narayan

Patna, Nov. 11—

"It is clear from what I have been able to gather that the terrible and gruesome things that happened in Bihar are to the eternal shame of the province and of the majority community here. The majority community of Bihar have been guilty of heinous crimes and have committed deeds of abject cowardice and barbarity." Thus states Mr. Jayprakash Narayan, Member, Congress Working Committee, Leader of the Congress Socialist Party, in connection with the communal situation in Bihar.

He also said : "It is clear that the Noakhali tragedy has turned the entire province, particularly rural areas, into a veritable ammunition dump. It is so clear that the ignition has been supplied by various factors such as communalists, provocateurs and elements of every type. There are indications that big zamindars with vested interests threatened had a hand in the disturbances and also that the British and communal elements in services fished freely in troubled waters."

Concluding Mr. Jayprakash Narayan said : "I wish to warn people of the provice that we are not yet out of danger that Congressmen and other agencies working for peace must not relax or slow down their activities yet I appeal particularly to young men and students to do all they can to restore peace in the province and bring the two communities together. I want everyone to remember that the present riots are part of the British plan to impede and obstruct India's progress.

(Star of India, Calcutta, 12.11.46)
—U.P.I.

APPENDIX-III

"What Is Happening in Bihar is Terrible"
"Hardly Believe that Human Beings Can Behave So"

—Pandit Nehru

Patna, November 5—

Pandit Jawahar Lal Nehru, in course of statement says—"What has happened and is happening in certain parts of Bihar is terrible and I can hardly believe that human beings can behave so. We have to put an end to this madness immediately and then we can argue about it later. Any person who minimizes the gravity of the situation here does no service."

(The Statesman, Calcutta, Nov. 6, 1946)

APPENDIX-IV

"Appaling Things Done in Bihar."
Government Interference In Transmission of News

The Statesman, dated Calcutta, November 6, 1946, in its article under caption "Bihar" writes :

> "For years, Bihar has had bad repute as one of India's more disorderly provinces. Derailment of trains, with other forms of railway crime, have since the early thirties been endemic. Only recently, Mr. Gandhi deplored reports which had reached him of widespread rural lawlessness. These were confirmed by contributions to our correspondence column, and private and published accounts from many sources. For supposed political ends appling things were done in the province in August, 1942. During the last fortnight appaling things have evidently been done again this time for communal ends; and particulars about them have been notably slow in emergence, partly no doubt because of poor communications, but partly, it is alleged because of Governmental interference with message transmitted.".

(The Statesman, 6th November, 1946)

APPENDIX-V

"*HORRIBLE STENCH*"

"It is a Shame that Women & Children Have Been Done To Death *In a Most Brutal Manner*"

—Frontier Gandhi

Patna Jan. 17—

Khan Abdul Ghaffar Khan, Frontier Gandhi, the Congress leader of the N.W. Frontier, while on his tour of the riot affected villages in Bihar, visited Kanchanpur where he saw some wells filled with dead bodies and with a layer of earth on top, from which a horrible stench emanated. The Havildar of the armed police informed him that the village was raided by mobs from the west and south. The mobs killed a large number of people.

"To protect and save and not to kill is true religion", said Abdul Ghaffar Khan, visibly moved at the sight, "It is a shame that women and children have been done to death in a most brutal manner. It is a heinous crime. Those who have done this are enemies of the people, of the country, of the freedom of India and of mankind."

(U.P.I.)

Morning News, Calcutta, dated 18th January, 1917)

APPENDIX-VI

Noakhali and Bihar A Comparison
Bengal Premier's Letter to Malik Firoz Khan Noon

Bengal Secretariat
Writers' Buildings, Calcutta
30th November, 1946

My Dear Firoz,

If you would like to know what the Bengal Government is doing regarding Noakhali, I will try and put down on record some of the main points. As, however, I am dictating without any papers before me, I am not quite certain whether catalogue will be entire. Before I proceed, however. I should point out that there is a wide disparity between Noakhali and Bihar incidents. A mountain has been made of a molehill regarding Noakhali by the Hindu press and by the continued presence of Mr. Gandhi at the place who has realised that the position of Hindus can well be precarious in a huge Muslim majority area, but who does not apparently realise that the position of Muslims is still more precarious in Hindu majority areas. I say still more precarious on comparing the manner in which the Muslim majority had dealt with the Hindu minority in Noakhali and the manner in which the Hindu majority has dealt with Muslim minority in Bihar. In Noakhali two districts were nominally affected—actually two Thanas in each district were affected. In Bihar I understand that as many as six districts were affected. In Noakhali and Tippera taken together the verified figures of deaths are 139.

If you add to them all the apprehensions of the Hindus, they would not come to more than 200. In Bihar I think the minimum will be 30,000 and if you add the apprehensions of the Muslims, it will be something in the region of 40,000 to 50,000. In Noakhali we cannot trace any outrage on women. A great deal was made of it in the beginning. All the Hindu papers and organisations talked about rape and abductions and forcible marriages. It has been found that all cases of rape and abduction are based purely on hearsy and not a single case has yet been brought to the notice of the authorities. The Muslim menfolk have behaved very honourably towards the Hindu women. There have been two or three cases at the most of marriages which are called 'forcible' but actually these marriages took place after conversion, and there have been many cases of reciprocal marriages, that is to say, the Muslims have given their girls in marriage into the family of the converted Hindus. You can quite see that the things are not so horrible as they are painted. Wherever Mr. Gandhi goes, however, a number of tales and stories are brought before him. The Hindu volunteers go first as scouts and try to get the Hindus to place before him false tales. I think that Mr. Gandhi has realised that the tales are exaggerated and false and he has the greatest difficulty in arriving at the substratum of truth. Now what have we done regarding this?

APPENDIX VII

The following is the verbatim copy of the Morning News Report of 20th Oct. 1946, regarding Fatwa Meeting :

Leader Tells Bihar Hindus To Attack Muslims. "Congress Government Will Secretly Help Us."

Fatwa Oct. 19—

"We are determined to destroy our enemies wherever they are in a minority. The Congress Government would connive at our action and help us strictly in all possible ways. Take it from me, that you will not be arrested and even if you are, you would be let off with very simple punishment."

This is what a prominent Hindu Congress Worker, deputed by Dr. Rajendra Prasad is reported to have told a gathering of Hindus at the Fatwa High English School, Patna, on September 27.

The following is the text of the speech, openly inciting Hindus to violence :

"Dear students and teachers—I am one of the 86 persons deputed by Dr. Rajendra Prasad for the uplift of the nation. First I want to let you know our history. Those who demand Pakistan deny that India is the homeland of the Aryans. The excavations of Mohanjo Daro reveal and the Vedas affirm that such assertions are wrong. Deeds of our bravery are recorded in the Ramayana and the Mahabharata.

"When we grew weak, jackals and asses from Arabia came and grew fat on our spoils. When they were satiated they gave to the vulture from the Thames. The cumulative effect of all these was the utter ruin of the motherland.

"The Ramayana mentions of a herb which makes a dead man alive. Gandhiji, Rajendra Babu and other leaders used that life-giving herb for the rebirth of the Hindu nation and today we find ourselves alive.

"You must not forget what the Arab asses did to us. They conquered our country and slaughtered our brave soldiers. Mahmud Ghuznavi sacked the beautiful cities of India and carried the booty to Ghazana. Alauddin's rape of Rajputana is well known. Akbar also did a great harm to us. But these reached their climax during the reign of Aurangzeb. He forced the Hindus to accept Islam and those who refused were drowned in boiling water.

"Dear boys, do we not feel taking revenge? This is the right time for us to destroy and annihilate our enemies. We must devote ourselves whole-heartedly to this job. The Congress Government shall be conniving at our actions and shall be helping us secretly in all possible ways. We are determined to destory our enemies wherever they are in a minority. Take it from me that you people shall not be arrested and even if you are arrested you shall get very simple punishment.

"An association has been formed at Dinapur for imparting military education to the Hindus. I request you people to join this military training centre. First let us establish our Government in India and after that we have to conquer Iran and Arabia."

(Morning News—Dated Calcutta, the 20th Oct. 1946)
(Also reported in Sada-i-Am, Patna of 9.10.46)

Bibliography

(A) Published and Unpublished Govt. Records

1. Political Special File No. 1346/1916.
2. Political Special File No. 1165/1916.
3. Political Special File No. 216/1917.
4. Political Special File No. 112/1917.
5. Political Special File No. 421/1919.
6. Political Special File No. 172/1923.
7. Political Special File No. 173/1923.
8. Political Special File No. 1/1923.
9. Political Special File No. 51/1925.
10. Political Special File No. 271/1925.
11. Political Special File No. 216/1927.
12. Political Special File No. 92/1928.
13. Political Special File No. 106/1928.
14. Political Special File No. 111/1928.
15. Political Special File No. 23/1929.
16. Political Special File No. 115/1931.
17. Political Special File No. 30/1932, Part II.
18. Political Special File No. 18/1933.
19. Political Special File No. 69/1933.
20. Political Special File No. 217/1933.
21. Political Special File No. 182/1933.
22. Political Special File No. 16/1938.
23. Political Special File No. 584/1939.
24. Political Special File No. 110/1940.
25. Political Special File No. 400/1947.

26. **Political** Special File No. 2665/1947.
27. **Political** Special File No. 209/1947.
28. **Political** Special File No. 247/1947.
29. **Political** Special File No. 578/1947.
30. **Political** Special File No. 250/1947.
31. **Political** Special File No. 319/1947.
32. **Political** Special File No. 317/1947.
33. **Political** Special File No. 452/1947.

(B) **Fortnightly Report to the Govt. of Bihar & Orissa,** 3rd February 1940.

2. do 20th April 1940.
3. do 5th May 1951.
4. do 16th November 1946.

(C) **Bihar and Orissa Folice Abstract of Intelligence,** 1912.

2. do 1913.
3. do 1914.
4. do 1915.
5. do 1916.
6. do 1917.

(D) **Administrative Report to the Govt. of Bihar and Orissa,** 1923-24.

2. Administrative Report 1924-25.
3. Administrative Report 1926-27.
4. Administrative Report 1927-28.
5. Administrative Report 1928-29.
6. Administrative Report 1929-30.
7. Administrative Report 1930-31.
8. Administrative Report 1931-32.
9. Administrative Report 1932-34.

(E) **District Gazetteers**

1. L.S.S.O'Malley, *District Gazetteer, Saran,* (Calcutta, 1908).
2. L.S.S.O.'Malley, *Bihar and Orissa District Gazetteer, Saran,* (Calcutta, 1924).
3. L.S.S.O.'Malley, *Bengal District Gazetteer, Muzaffarpur,* (Calcutta, 1907).
4. L.S.S.O.'Malley, *Bihar and Orissa District Gazetteer, Patna,* (Calcutta, 1924).

5. L.S.S.O.'Malley, *Shahabad District Gazetteer* (Calcutta, 1924).

(F) **Report of the Indian Statutory Commission,** Vol. I, II, III & IV, (Calcutta, 1930).

G) **Political Police Proceeding** 1891-95.

(H) **The Bihar State Killing** (1946).

Published Official Statement and Resolution of the Bihar *Provincial Muslim League.*

NEWSPAPERS & MAGAZINES

1. The Behar Herald, (Weekly from Patna), dated Dec. 5, 1912.
2. The Behar Herald, December 11, 1915.
3. The Behar Herald, January 15, 1916.
4. The Behar Herald, October 13, 1917.
5. The Behar Herald, November 10, 1917.
6. The Behar Herald, January 6, 1923.
7. The Behar Herald, September 14, 1923.
8. The Behar Herald, June 7, 1924.
9. The Behar Herald, September 19, 1925.
10. The Behar Herald, July 24, 1926.
11. The Behar Herald, September 25, 1926.
12. The Behar Herald, July 30, 1927.
13. The Behar Herald, May 28, 1930.
14. The Behar Herald, September 29, 1934.

(ii) The Mirror.
(iii) The Young India,
(iv) The Searchlight
(v) The Indian Nation.
(vi) Tarun Bharat
(vii) Liberty
(viii) The Times of India
(ix) Amrit Bazar Patrika.
(x) The Aryavarta.
(xi) The Mainstream
(xii) The Social Scientist
(xiii) Tribune.

BOOKS

Ahmed, Sufia, *Muslim Community in Bengal*, (Dacca, 1974).

Ali, Mohammad, *Selected Writings and Speeches*, (Lahore, 1944), edited by Iqbal.

Ahmed, M. *Responsible Government and the Solution of Hindu-Muslim Problem*, (London, 1928).

Agrawala, R.M. *The Hindu-Muslim Riots : Their causes and cures*, (Lucknow, 1943).

Ambedkar, B.R., *Pakistan or the Partition of India*, (Bombay, 1946) 3rd edn.

Amery, L.S. *India and Freedom* (London, 1942).

Aziz, K.K., *Britain and Muslim India*, (London, 1963).

Azad, Maulana Abul Kalam, *India Wins Freedom*, (Bombay, 1959). Reprint.

Ansari, M.A. *Muslims and the Congress: Select Correspondence 1912-1935*, edited by M. Hasan, (New Delhi, 1979).

Bahadur, L. *The Muslim League : Its History, Activities and Achievements*, (Agra, 1954).

Bapat, M.S., *Nationalism Vs Communalism—An Essay on Hindu-Muslim unity*, (Poona, 1943 3rd ed.).

Bayly, C.A., *Rulers, Townsmen and Bazars*, (Cambridge, 1983).

Barrier, N.G. (ed.) *Roots of Communal Politics* (Delhi, 1976).

Bondurant, Joan, (ed.), *Harijan* in 19 Volumes, Published both from Newyork and London in 1973.

Broomfield, J.H., *Elite conflict in a Plural Society : Twentieth Century Bengal*, (Berkeley, 1968).

Chand, S.M. *National Leaders on Communalism*, (Jaipur, 1985).

Chandra, Bipan, *Communalism in Modern India*, (New Delhi, 1984).

———, *Modern India*, (Delhi, 1977).

———, *Nationalism and Colonialism in Modern India*, (New Delhi, 1979).

———, *Communalism and the Writings of Indian History*, (New Delhi, 1981).

Chandra, Satish, *Communal Interpretation of Indian History*, New Delhi, no date.

Chandra, Sudhir, "Communal consciousness in Late 19th Century Hindi literature" in M. Hasan (ed), *Communal and Pan-Islamic Trends in Colonial India*, (New Delhi, 1981).

Choudhary, V.C.P., *Secularism Versus Communalism*, (Patna, 1977).

Choudhary, Valmiki (ed), *Dr. Rajendra Prasad Correspondence and Select Documents* (New Delhi, 1984).

Curran, J.A. *Militant Hinduism in Indian Politics*, (New Delhi, 1979), reprint.

Desai, A.R., *Social background of Indian Nationalism*, (Bombay, 1959), 3rd edition.

Dixit, Prabha, *Communalism—A struggle for Power*, (New Delhi, 1974).

Durrani, F.K. Khan, *The Meaning of Pakistan*, (Lahore, 1944).

Dutt, R. Palme, *India Today*, (Bombay, 1949) revised edn.

David Page, *Prelude to Partition*, (Oxford, 1982).

Engineer, A.A., *On Developing Theory of Communal Riots* (Bombay, 1984).

Ghurye, G.S., *Social Tensions in India*, (Bombay, 1968).

Gandhi, M.K *The way to Communal Harmony*, (Ahmedabad, 1963).

———, *Collected works*, (New Delhi, 1958).

———, *Communal unity*, (Ahmedabad, 1949).

Gopal, Ram, *Indian Muslims : A Political History* 1858-1947), (Bombay, 1959).

Gopal. S. *British Policy in India 1858-1905*, (New Delhi, 1975).

———, *Jawaharlal Nehru—A Biography* 1889-1947, Vol. one, (London, 1975).

Houser, W. 'The Provincial Kisan Sabha 1929-1942, A study of Indian Peasant Movement,' a dissertation submitted for Ph.D. in Chicago University (1961). The book remains unpublished today.

Hodson, H.V., *The Great Divide*, (New York, 1971).

Hasan, M., *Communal and Pan-Islamic Trends in Colonial India*, (New Delhi, 1981).

Husain, S. Abid, *The Destiny of Indian Muslims*, (Bombay, 1965).

Jinnah, M.A., *Speeches and Writings*, two volumes edited by Jamil-ud-Din Ahmed, (Lahore, 1964) edn.

Kabir, Humayun, *Minorities in Democracy* (Calcutta, 1968).

———, *Muslim Politics 1906-1942*, (Calcutta, 1943).

Kumar, Akhilesh, 'Socio-economic base of communal riots in India, a brief survey 1890-1948 in Proceeding of the *Indian History Congress*, (Burdwan, 1983).

Krishna, K.B. *The Problem of Minorities*, (London, 1939).

K. Mark and F. Engels, Selected Works, Vol. I, (Masco, 1977).

Lyall, A.C. *Asiatic Studies : Religious and Social*, (London, 1884), edn. 2.

Mazumdar, R.C., *History of Freedom Movement*, (Calcutta, 1962).

Maclane, J.R., *Indian Nationalism and the Early Congress*, (Princeton, 1977).

Mishra, B.B. ed), *Mahatma Gandhi's Movement in Champaran*, (Patna, 1963).

M. Hasan (ed), *Muslims and the Congress*, (Delhi, 1978).

Mangalori, T.A. *Musalman Ka Roshan Mustaqbil*, (Urdu), (Delhi, 1945).

Narayan, Shriman (Compiled), *Gandhiji's Selected Letters*, (Ahmedābad, 1968).

Nehru, Jawaharlal, *An Autobiography*, (New Delhi, 1962), reprint.

———, *A Bunch of Old Letters*, (Bombay, 1958).

———, *Selected Works* edited by S. Gopal, (New Delhi, 1972).

———, *The Discovery of India*, (London, 1946).

———, *Recent Essays and Writings : On the Future of Indian Communalism and other* subjects, (Allahabad, 1934).

Jawaharlal Nehru on Communalism, edited by M.L. Gupta, (New Delhi, 1934).

Prasad, Bimal, *The Hindu-Muslim Question*, (Allahabad, 1941).

———, "British Attitude Towards the Communal Problem in India", mimeograph presented at the Seminar on "The

Communal Problem in India 1919" Organised by the Nehru Memorial Museum and Library, New Delhi, in March 1971.

Prasad, Rajendra, *India Divided*, (Bombay, 1947), 3rd revised edn.

———, *Autobiography*, (Bombay, 1957).

Pandey, B.N. (ed), *The Indian National Movement 1885-1947* : Select Documents, (Delhi, 1979).

Padmasha, *Indian National Congress and Muslims*, (New Delhi, 1980).

Pirzada, S.S., *Foundations of Pakistan*, (Karachi, 1970).

Patwardhan, A. and A. Mehta, *The Communal Triangle in India* (Allahabad, 1947).

Rajput, A.B., *Muslim League : Yesterday and Today*, (Lahore, 1948).

Rai, Amrit (ed), *Vividh Prasang* (Hindi), (Allahabad, 1975).

Rude, George, *Crowds in History 1730-1848*, (New York, 1964).

Sarkar, Sumit, *Modern India 1885-1947*, (New Delhi, 1983).

Sayeed, K.B., *Pakistan : A Formative Phase*, (Karachi, 1968).

Sharma, R.S. *Ancient India*, (New Delhi, 1977).

Sharma, Ramvilas, *Bharat Mein Angrezi Raj aur Marxvad* (Hindi), in two Volumes, (New Delhi, 1982).

Sewak, Ram, *History of Bihar between Two World Wars*, (New Delhi, 1985).

Shah, C.G. *Marxism Gandhism Stalinism*, (Bombay, 1963).

Srinivas, M.N., *Social Change in Modern India*, New Delhi, 1966).

Thursby, G.R. *Hindu-Muslim Relations in British India*, (Leiden, 1975).

Yasin, Mohammad, *A Social History of Islamic India*, (Lahore, 1958).

Index

N

P

R

S

T

U

W

Y

Z